Journey to
Wholeness

Journey to Wholeness

Healing body, mind and soul

Thomas D. Maddix and Ian C. Soles

NOVALIS

© 2003 Novalis, Saint Paul University, Ottawa, Canada

Cover: Caroline Gagnon
Cover images: (front cover) Getty Images; (author photographs) Chris White
Layout: Caroline Gagnon and Francine Petitclerc

Business Office:
Novalis
49 Front Street East, 2nd Floor
Toronto, Ontario, Canada
M5E 1B3

Phone: 1-800-387-7164 or (416) 363-3303
Fax: 1-800-204-4140 or (416) 363-9409
E-mail: cservice@novalis.ca
www.novalis.ca

National Library of Canada Cataloguing in Publication

Maddix, Thomas D., 1946–
    Journey to wholeness : healing body, mind and soul / Thomas D.
Maddix and Ian C. Soles.

Includes bibliographical references.
ISBN 2-89507-247-7

    1. Spirituality. 2. Healing–Religious aspects–Christianity. I. Soles, Ian C.
II. Title.

BT732.5.M348 2003   234'.131   C2003-900374-4

Printed in Canada.

We acknowledge the financial support of the Government of Canada
through the Book Publishing Industry Development Program (BPIDP)
for our publishing activities.

5   4   3   2   1   07   06   05   04   03

Acknowledgments

The authors would like to acknowledge the following individuals for their comments and direction in the preparation of this book:

George Klawitter CSC, Ph.D., St. Edward University, Austin, TX
Dr. Joan Neehall, Edmonton, AB
Dr. Mary Kathryn Grant, Michigan City, IN
Philip Armstrong CSC, Notre Dame, IN
Frank Rotsaert CSC, Sienna Heights University, Adrian, MI
Joseph McTaggart CSC, Columba Hall, Notre Dame, IN
Don Ruzicka, Killam, AB
Ken Bradley, Edmonton, AB
Ayalah Aylyn, Edmonton, AB
Katie Soles, Edmonton, AB
Martin Hovestad, Edmonton, AB

In particular, Ian would like to thank his clients who trusted him with their story and invited him to partake in their journey. He also recognizes the important contribution of his teachers, Rob Farrar-Koch, Dr. Amy Lu, Maggie Hodgson, Robert Harris and Hildegard Wittlinger. Especially, Ian wishes to express his love and gratitude to his wife, Katie, who consistently leads him to live deeply in the sacred, seeking compassion and thoughtfulness, and to their daughter, Natasha, without whom the path of massage therapy would likely never have opened.

Tom and Ian would also like to extend their gratitude to Novalis, particularly Kevin Burns and Anne Louise Mahoney, for their faith in our work, their patience, and their craft.

Contents

Note to the Reader

During a three-hour drive back to Edmonton from Jasper National Park in western Canada, the dream for this book emerged.

We come from distinct backgrounds. Ian is a husband, father and massage therapist. Tom, a member of the Roman Catholic order of men known as the Brothers of Holy Cross, is a vice-president of a health group, consultant with faith-based health organizations and teacher of spirituality. Given the diversity of our life experiences, we decided to find a way to share some of our insights from our own journeys and those of the people who have entered our lives.

Telling good stories and giving personal commentary on them has been at the heart of human communication forever. Stories often reveal how we integrate, or fail to integrate, fragments of our lives. Many of us look to a story or a piece of literature, a movie or a television drama not only for entertainment but also to catch glimpses of understanding about ourselves, others and all Creation. Whether the story is Homer's *Odyssey* or a contemporary love story, the human heart seeks images to guide it through and make sense of life's vicissitudes. Sometimes we are fortunate enough to find an image that both enriches and expands our lives. On other occasions, we fall prey to a life image that diminishes us, and in so doing diminishes the world around us. Yet we continue to search for meaning and wholeness – in our lives and in our society.

Surprises await – just as they did for the Greek wanderer Odysseus and for the movie character Forrest Gump. The journey through life is filled with disappointments, the unexpected turns along the way that bring us to a greater sense of ourselves and others. At some points we feel alienated, alone and confused. But wherever we find ourselves, we strive to make sense of what we experience. Sometimes this can only happen when we are willing to tell our stories to one another, in order to see where pain and joy reside. Sometimes it's only through pain that our soul can reconnect with the sacred that lives deep within. Again and again we ask, "Why me?" or "Why us?" These enduring questions find resolution in the human heart through the stories we employ to give meaning and purpose to our deepest longings.

Self-knowledge, which is often acquired only after much pain, searching and confusion, provides the key to understanding both inner and outer quests. We come to realize that the longing for wholeness comes from within; it cannot be found outside ourselves. The turning point arrives at different times for different people. We might spend all our days fighting the demons of life, or befriend them and discover that they can help us understand the mystery of Creation as well as the complexity or simplicity of our lives. The struggle between surrendering to the "gold," the sacred mystery within, and resisting the inward journey with constant activity, scapegoating or fear lies at the centre of our desire for wholeness.

It helps to remember that we are not alone. Fellow travellers can guide us if we open ourselves to their companionship and experience. The great religious traditions of the world talk about a loving and compassionate God who dwells in each of us and in the world around us. Our task is to discover people who are our kindred spirits in whatever way they reveal themselves, and to awaken to the hidden presence of the sacred.

This book seeks to explore the interconnectedness of mind, body and soul through a series of reflections on spirituality, the personal stories of people who have sought massage therapy from Ian, and Tom's insights about the people who have entered his life. In each, we seek to understand how to open ourselves to the deepest longings of mind, body and soul in our quest for wholeness. TV commentator Bill Moyers concludes an essay from his book *Healing and the Mind* with these powerful words: "Healing begins with caring. So does civilization."[1] We, as authors, promote healing, caring and creating a world grounded in hope.

When we speak of healing, we mean a sense of well-being and wholeness. We do not mean cure of illness or disease, but a sense of acceptance. Healing brings the fragments of our life together as a whole, and frees our spirits to be about their business.

Tom writes the first part of each chapter writes the personal stories and reflections base experience as a massage therapist. Two exceptio format exist. Tom has written Chapter 1, "The Longing," and Ian has written Chapter 10, "Healing as a Community."

At the end of each chapter we offer questions to facilitate ongoing discussion or personal reflection. The book's three sections encourage the reader to explore the longing for wholeness individually or within a group.

We hope that you find yourselves among these stories, as we have.

Tom Maddix and Ian Soles

Part One

Opening
to the Experience

Chapter 1

The Longing

God, You are my God, I am seeking you,
my soul is thirsting for you,
my flesh is longing for you,
a land parched, weary and waterless...

— *Psalm 63:1*

There is no role that absolves us of the responsibility to
listen, to be mindful that life is all around us, touching us.

— *Rachel Remen, MD*

Meditation is a medium, like a chariot, by which we
bypass the intellect and enter the great ocean of awareness
that resides within us all and that is one and the same with
universe and infinity.

— *Avram Davis and Manuela D. Mascot*

Who among us does not want to be whole? We may
not always be able to articulate our desire, but
something within nudges us to seek a greater sense of
well-being. We acknowledge this urge when we meet
people who complement us and enable us to experience
a deeper sense of soul. We know it in the impulse to buy
something we believe will enable us to feel better, more

at ease with ourselves. And we intuit it when we know that something – a relationship, position or belonging – that keeps us from being who we long to become must be shed.

During a recent visit, my friend Therese mentioned that after almost 20 years of marriage she had just moved out of the house. When I asked why, she said her loneliness has increased over the years and she felt her very being was dying. The abrupt decision to leave shocked her husband and children. Despite a long series of arguments, her husband did not realize the depth of her pain and unfulfillment until he and Therese met with a counsellor. What Therese and her husband had hoped to be a path of wholeness – a marriage and family – had turned into a journey of decay and diminishment for all involved.

The desire for wholeness sometimes takes us on paths that involve considerable pain, that demand letting go and grieving before healing and wholeness start to emerge. The journey requires patience, perseverance, faith in the ultimate goodness of life and a willingness to learn from our experiences. In terms of spirituality, world faith traditions provide not only a framework in which to envision a harmonius life but also a meeting place and source of healing. Within the Christian tradition, the Scriptures are filled with stories of healing and transformation. Jesus reveals himself as a healer in his ability to touch, listen and respond to people's depths. The same is true in other traditions.

For instance, the sixteenth-century Carmelite Brother Lawrence, a cook for his Catholic order, created a series of maxims. In one of his reflections, he talks about the "hidden spark" of God who lives deep within our hearts.

> During our work and other activities, and even during our times of reading or writing, even though they be spiritually orientated – and yes, even more during our outward devotions and prayers aloud – we ought to stop for a short moment, as frequently as we can, to adore God deep within our hearts and take pleasure in Him…. Since you are not unmindful of the fact that God is present before you as you carry out your duties, and you know that He is at the depth and centre of your soul, why not stop from time to time, whatever you are doing – even if you are praying aloud – to adore Him inwardly, to praise Him, to beseech Him, to offer your heart to Him, and to thank Him?[2]

Many people today have lost the experience of a living God dwelling deep inside us. Instead, we often dismiss the inner life and seek assurance only in what can be proven by reason. Likewise, many fear the power of the living God as a source of healing and transformation. We just don't believe that a compassionate God could care about our journey and us!

In Jewish spirituality, a wonderful cosmology was developed by the sixteenth-century kabbalistic rabbi Isaac Luria. In his view, at the beginning of the world there was Or Ein Sof, a pure and absolute being. The world as we know it was created when the Or Ein Sof, an emanation of light from the Absolute Source, was involved in an accident of cosmic proportions.

According to his theory, the vessel containing the light of Or Ein Sof shattered, and the light of God was scattered throughout the universe in an infinite number of holy sparks hidden deep in everyone and everything.

Like creation stories of other traditions, this one expresses the desire to create a better world and restore humanity to wholeness. It declares that the purpose of life is to uncover the sparks of light and restore the world to its original state. Everyone and everything we encounter is a container for holiness that we must help to set free. The kabbalah talks then of Tikkun Olam, the repair and the restoration of the world.

These two examples, which are present in other traditions as well, tell us that God wants us to be in contact with God, but also wants us to be whole. Yet, to be whole, we need to make a conscious choice – as Therese did with her marriage. We can stop whatever we are doing at a given moment and speak with God who is living inside our hearts, as Brother Lawrence instructs, or we can seek to find the hidden sparks of divine love in everyone and everything, as the kabbalah suggests. The challenge is also the source of the longing within us; we are individuals, as well as people hungering for holiness and wholeness.

We also live as part of a larger community of people and events. What diminishes or heals one person also diminishes or heals a community. Just as families, co-workers and neighbours are interconnected, so are we. While at times we may feel solitary, life around us continues to challenge, enlighten and influence our well-being. In other words, life becomes a laboratory for self-discovery and healing. Whether we find ourselves in the wrong line at the grocery store checkout, working in an area filled with toxic waste, or immersed in a caring community, life continually touches us.

This laboratory reveals our longings as individuals and communities. We cannot isolate ourselves from suffering, illness, love and beauty – whether it's directed to individuals or communities. The longing for wholeness has an impact on the lives of those around us. I'm reminded of this each morning, when street people or self-employed individuals visit the dumpster outside the complex where I live. Sometimes I have started to toss my garbage into the dumpster only to encounter a head looking up at me from inside. At other times, someone steps back as I toss in the garbage. This shows me that many members of our society continue to suffer from hunger, homelessness, deprivation and often-untreated pain and suffering.

I believe transformation starts from within and moves outward. It starts with individuals who acknowledge their pain, as well as their blessedness, and thus change the way they live and act. I remember working with a group a number of years ago that found itself in a very uneasy situation. While the group's members had hoped for others to continue to join them, that didn't happen. When people came, they departed within a short period of time. Some key members also moved on, leaving the remaining members sad and confused. We worked with the pain, some of it very up-front and some stored deep. It became clear that someone had to be willing to surrender to the moment and to go into the darkness, to see where new life existed not only for himself or herself but also for the group. Yet there was tremendous resistance to going into the darkness. Most group members opted to find short-term solutions, scapegoat others or make life miserable for those who wanted to grow and develop. For many, the fear of losing "control" of the world they knew was overwhelming.

I remember a psychologist reminding the group that as one person changed, everyone had to change because the way members related to one another in the past would no longer do. It would only hurt the individual who was trying to heal – and the group would also suffer. Yet healing requires a willingness to let go of actions, attitudes and values that no longer give life and energy. While this is easy to write or say, it's much harder to actualize. One person referred to a segment of this group as the "walking dead," and he was right. These people formed a kind of subgroup that had taken on its own personality where repressed anger, resentment and fear paralyzed and killed the human spirit. Of course, those who sought to change and heal were vilified for trying to get on with their lives.

Healing, whether personal, familial or collective, always demands a price. It requires that we give up something – an attitude, a stance towards someone or something, a relationship – in order to embrace something more whole and life-giving. We all know there will be a cost, but being willing to name it and pay it provides the avenue to wholeness. We also know that sometimes we are able to move, while at other times we remain stuck. We say, "I can't do that now, wait awhile."

Healing happens because we open ourselves to the longing for wholeness, and respond to it. It may not take the shape we think it will, but it *does* happen because it flows from the river of life deep inside.

The experiences of daily living – all those ups and downs that affect us consciously or unconsciously – provide the framework in which our personal and collective story emerges. In it we may freely engage the forces we encounter, or we may flee. However, if we run away, wholeness cannot emerge. If we are to be whole, we must face the darkness, risk the encounters with evil. Only then can we say that we have become conversant with the longing deep in our souls for meaning and connectedness to something much larger than ourselves. As Teresa of Avila said in the sixteenth century, "For the most part, all our trials and disturbances come from our *not* knowing ourselves."

Questions for Reflection

- How does longing for wholeness reveal itself in my life?

- How do I block this longing?

- What are two ways I can nurture this longing?

- How do I make time to relate to the Divine within?

- In what ways have I recently noticed the hidden sparks of holiness in the world and people around me?

Chapter 2

Finding Our Path

We all have within us a centre of stillness, surrounded by silence.

— *Dag Hammarskjöld*

If you do not express your own original ideas, if you do not listen to your own being, you will have betrayed yourself.

— *Rollo May*

Any discussion of spirituality and healing flows from the belief that the sacred lives within us, at the very core of our being. Without this central belief, or a desire for it, our quest for healing loses direction and gets distracted by all the things around us. Maybe the hardest journey we ever undertake is the journey to the core of our being to be greeted and embraced by the love of the sacred. It's a pilgrimage of awe, mystery, surrender and uncertainty.

In reflecting upon spirituality and healing, it's important to be clear about our terms. A definition of spirituality that I heard many years ago has stayed with me: spirituality is the glue that holds us together. It is the longing within us that connects us to the sacred, a mystery that binds us to self, others, nature and the universe.

A number of years ago, in a university course entitled "Theology and Community Service," students visited two residents at a nursing home weekly for one semester. During many discussions about healing and spirituality, one student spoke with a woman who had made a pilgrimage to Lourdes, in southwest France. Lourdes has been a major pilgrimage destination for Catholics and others since 1858, when a young girl named Bernadette Soubirous had a series of visions of Mary, the mother of God. When asked by the Virgin Mary to dig into the ground with her hands, Bernadette discovered a stream – and since that moment Lourdes has been recognized as a place of healing and occasional cure. People come from around the world to participate in prayers, processions and immersions into the healing waters. The strength of the moment flows not only from the encounter with the sacred but also from the energy and desire of the sick, the broken and their families and friends who seek healing. When a student asked the nursing home resident if she had been cured at Lourdes, she replied, "No, but I have come to a new meaning in my life and I am prepared to go on with the next stage."

Healing happened for this woman, and everyone in the class learned something very important. It is the inner intention we bring to the process of healing that provides the deeper meaning we seek.

What happens as we open ourselves to healing and the sacred? I sense that there is a letting go – of images of self, others, God and a life that no longer make sense to us. A friend of mine, talking about his troubled relationship with his father, said: "I finally came to realize that he did the best he could as a widower at 35 with small children. My anger came from within me, and from my unmet expectations. Now that I have forgiven him and let go of my unreal expectations, I am more peaceful and open to a relationship with him."

Psychiatrist Carl Jung once remarked that "spirituality is the soul in search of its proper path." I know from my own experience and from the audiences with whom I have shared this definition that it makes sense. Jung felt deeply about the power of the unconscious and soul to heal itself; his writing invites us to discover the core of our being and embrace it. Many of us play a dodging game with the soul. We sense it stirring deep within through various intuitions, tugs at our conscience and dreams. Yet, while we desire the wholeness that comes from walking our proper path, the journey to wholeness often strips away images that have shaped our understanding of ourselves and others. We find ourselves resisting the very thing we desire.

The American psychologist James Hollis writes in his probing book, *Swamplands of the Soul*, that "most of us were conditioned to be nice rather than real, accommodating rather than authentic and adaptive rather than assertive."[3] When we put Jung's notion of spirituality next to Hollis' observations about human life, we can better focus upon the texture of our journey and all its complexities. Clearly, we must acknowledge and shed the subtle conditioning that has shaped us so thoroughly before we can begin.

Recently, I conducted a group exercise using fantasy. Participants were invited to identify one thing or value that they need right now, and to articulate its "cost." In this particular group, most said that they were not willing to pay the estimated "cost." Why? As the group's members talked about their resistance, a clear clash emerged between professional goals and personal values. For them, professional goals and rewards provided more stimuli for growth than did being on the path to wholeness. It was a sad, revealing moment.

Our life journey takes many twists, and sometimes we have the wrong glue. For many of us, the glue may be work, alcohol, sports, shopping, complaining, sex or unreflective religion. Ultimately, we find ourselves disconnected from our core, our soul. While we may feel "held together" by work, for instance, and cannot imagine life without it, on a deeper level there is a subtle voice asking, "Is that all there is?" Of course, when the voice tugs a little harder we can stop and listen or flee, only to become more stuck.

The inner tension caused by the struggle to follow our proper path and the path of living consciously or unconsciously provides the energy and framework for our spirituality. It also directs how we relate to self, God, others and Creation. As I have listened to people over the years, I have noticed that we live on many levels. In fact, often what we see is not the real person at all. The other day, a friend told me how people tend to characterize him as an aggressive athlete. While he is a superb athlete, he is also a person committed to reflection, relationships and knowing himself and the world better. Yet in the world of athletic competition, little room exists for a more in-depth portrayal. We often do not allow other people's full depth to emerge because it unnerves us. However, if we want to be whole and healthy, with an increasing ability to live with mystery, ambiguity and paradox, we need to allow ourselves and others to find their proper path and live it.

We'll never know how often we put up blocks to ourselves and others. I recall a woman from one class who was always upset that her spouse did not feel called to the same type of spiritual openness and exploration that she experienced. The more she tried to convince him to come along on the journey, the more he resisted. After years of suffering, she finally realized that we each have our own path to walk, and we cannot force another to come with us or do it for us. Honouring the soul is a solitary adventure that we undertake at our own peril or happiness. We discover the face of the sacred through a diversity of expression.

Deep within us lies a life-giving stillness that holds the key to who we are and where we are going. Throughout life, we often get lost as our energies turn towards the mundane stuff of daily life. Often we lose touch with the core of our being. The space of stillness and solitude lives within nonetheless. We can reach into it over and over, awakening the mystery of life and awe within us.

Leslie's Story

Leslie passed through my life in what seemed like a fleeting moment, but her presence has remained with me, not only because of her courage and resilience but also because of her deep hope. Her story underlines how an individual can come to accept a situation, even when fate brings an entirely unexpected challenge. Her life demonstrates how we can incorporate new circumstances into our being and carry on with what we feel called to do.

Leslie came to see me by chance after her friend found my name on the Internet in a list of manual lymph drainage (MLD) therapists. A regular client had cancelled an appointment so Leslie took it. When I heard her symptoms, I wondered if she had severe lymphedema, and how I would fit the necessary treatment plan into my busy schedule.

Lymphedema is a condition that results from a disruption to the normal flow of lymphatic fluid in the body. The disruption can cause severe swelling and, if left untreated, becomes extreme, as in the case of elephantiasis. The most common regions that swell are the arms and legs, although any area of the body can be affected. This is a chronic condition, so the only effective treatment is gentle (MLD) massage, compression bandaging and exercise until the affected areas have been returned to normal size. Following initial treatment, compression garments are worn to maintain the normal size of the limb.

Leslie arrived at our clinic with bilateral lymphedema in her arms, chest and back. She had been diagnosed with breast cancer months earlier while in Africa, where she and her husband worked for a non-governmental development agency. She had come to Halifax for a double radical mastectomy, chemotherapy and MLD therapy. After seven months in treatment, she stopped over in Edmonton to visit a friend before planning to travel the next day to meet her husband and two adopted children in Asia.

I discovered that she was not properly prepared by her cancer specialists to deal with the possibility of lymphedema in a developing country that lacked basic medical services, let alone MLD therapists to treat her. More importantly, I realized that she had put her illness and the subsequent complications of ongoing swelling in a workable context that enabled her to get on with her life. What Leslie was experiencing because of her cancer and lymphedema would be enough for most people to handle in a lifetime – never mind the complications of travelling halfway around the world to live and work.

Although our few hours together did not permit much time to discuss her perceptions, it was readily apparent that Leslie had her illness in a healthy context. She viewed herself as fortunate, given the circumstances, that she was able to travel to Canada for surgery, unlike the vast majority of women with whom she had worked, who often died without basic treatment.

Leslie seemed acutely aware of her path in life, and her place within something larger than herself. Although her pain and suffering were very real and life-threatening, she appeared comfortable and prepared to continue working to improve the lives of people caught in dire poverty. In the time I spent with her, I searched for a sense of denial. Instead, I found within Leslie a sense of peace with the unknown, and a woman who lives in the present while looking to the future. She took adversity in stride, acutely aware of her own situation but able to avoid getting entirely mired in pain and suffering.

Leslie and her husband now live and work in rural Asia. While she must modify some aspects of her life due to her ongoing condition, she still works to help others while caring for the needs of her family in conditions that would challenge the best of us.

For me, Leslie reflects what it means to have a sense of well-being and wholeness even in circumstances that may challenge one's very self. She showed me what it means to live from the core of one's soul, and taught me the power of knowing the "glue that holds us together" in the midst of complexity and uncertainty.

Leslie has not shared with me her beliefs or thoughts on life, spirituality, compassion or love. But the way she lives, the continued giving and sharing regardless of her own suffering, says more about her core beliefs, about the nature of her soul, than anything she could say. Leslie's journey shows what happens when we look outside ourselves and continue to engage life, while integrating our experiences. We push to become a whole person even when that person is different than the one we once knew.

Final Considerations

Finding our path takes us on roads we would never choose if we were not tossed there by fate or circumstance. In following it, we come to know the sacred within, and over time begin to discern what distracts us from the essence of our being. Let us look at the stories of Odysseus and Dante. Whether it be the curse of the god Poseidon, as in the case of Odysseus, or exile such as Dante suffered, achieving clarity and overcoming disorientation holds the possibility of genuine growth. When we know what is at the centre of our being and stay connected to it, we feel whole and secure. It is in clarifying which images make sense and sustain, and which ones distract and destroy, that we become ourselves. Life lived with meaning and purpose flows from connecting the various fragments of our life into a whole. Illness, joy, love and sorrow constitute the tests along the way. It is up to us to bring integration and meaning into the paths we walk.

In an interview with Bill Moyers, Rachel Naomi Remen, MD, when asked to comment on the fact that life is dangerous, said:

> ...my sense is that the worst thing that happens in life is not death. The worst thing would be to miss it. A friend of mine, Angeles Arien, says all spiritual paths have four steps: show up, pay attention, tell the truth and don't be attached to the results. I think the great danger in life is not showing up.[4]

Questions for Reflection

- What does spirituality mean to me?

- How is spirituality expressed and nurtured in my life?

- What image of the sacred lives deep within my soul?

- What questions about life does Leslie's experience raise for me?

- What in my life seeks healing at the present time? How does it manifest its desire?

- Where do I resist opening to the healing power within the core of my being? Why is this resistance present right now, and how does it manifest itself?

Part Two

Living the
Experience:
Images and Stories

Chapter 3

Unreflective Suffering

We saw nothing not because there was nothing, but because we had trained ourselves not to see.
— *Colm Toibin*

A warrior knows that war is made of many battles; he goes on.
— *Paulo Coelho*

"No pain, no gain!" How many times have we heard this slogan, and how many times have we lived it? I would bet that we have all swallowed our pride, gritted our teeth and endured unreflective and unnecessary suffering. While some suffering is unavoidable, I wonder why we often remain so married to our pain. Many athletes who are clearly in agony keep going. Many people stay in personal and work relationships that destroy their very dignity. Why is that? What is it about us that glorifies suffering to the point where we deny our very humanity? What images of self, others and Creation dominate our lives? What inner stories shape our existence? As the poet W.H. Auden sadly noted,

We would rather be ruined than changed:
We would rather die in our dread
Than climb the cross of the moment
And let our illusions die.[5]

Auden's observations about our stubborn ways reveal the power of inner stories to shape our lives. His comments also reveal the depth of our resistance to allowing our illusions to die or be altered. Many of us would rather die than confront our life-shaping inner stories, even if they are destructive or cause a great deal of suffering or physical discomfort.

Stories, like the hidden beams in a building, often provide a structure that supports our approach to self, others and the world around us. Tales of survival, heroism and vulnerability shape literature, lure us to the movies and provide an avenue by which we can enter into others' lives. They also provide images of what we interpret as "success" and a life well lived, what makes a good society, what values nurture it.

A wonderful teacher I had in university maintained that great literature, movies and drama provide a glimpse into human life and an enduring point of reference for us. But what happens when images and stories of unreflective heroism, unnecessary suffering and fear of appearing vulnerable shape our inner and outer worlds? Unfortunately, we often miss the core of our being and put ourselves into situations that damage not just ourselves but also those around us.

Spirituality invites us to shed the illusions that separate us from the sacred. The journey inward demands a willingness to pay the price for wholeness, balance and meaning. Yet meaning and balance do not emerge easily.

For many of us, those qualities emerge only through probing the darkness. By struggling with "demons" such as fear, insecurity and pride, which can lead us astray or hold us captive, we eventually discover a new integration about what constitutes a meaningful, whole life.

A major theme in spirituality is the invitation for a person to become aware of his or her interior dynamics and frees the seeker to live from his or her centre. In doing so, the person learns to listen to the prompting of the sacred deep within and to co-operate with these intuitions. For people who live in a state of unreflective suffering, this type of self-knowledge and responsibility is difficult. It demands a willingness to be vulnerable to personal weaknesses, demons, stories and images and to honour our gifts. It also requires a realization that something larger than self exists and demands respect.

Gandhi once said, "God speaks to us every day, only we do not know how to listen."[6] Gandhi's words capture the angst and suffering that ensue when deafness pervades our inner lives. When we fail to listen to the depths of our soul, we become like the warrior who allows everything to become a competition to be won. Unfortunately, self-knowledge and reflection have no place in this approach.

All the great religious traditions talk about letting go of control and inviting the Spirit into the broken, fragmented and wounded parts of self. The vulnerability needed in the spiritual journey goes against the loner mentality and "no pain, no gain" belief that one can conquer all by grit. Spirituality ultimately means surrendering to the love of God, who has called us into existence and seeks only our very best. Yet, if we fail to love others and be vulnerable and open to them, we cannot surrender to the loving power of the sacred.

Back in the fourth century, many people moved into the deserts of the upper Nile River area, in present-day Egypt, in order to reflect and get to know themselves, others and God better. While some returned quickly to the cities, others stayed in the desert and shared their learnings with those who came to them for guidance. One of the stories that emerged goes like this:

It was said about a disciple that he endured 70 weeks of fasting, eating only once a week. He asked God about certain words in the Holy Scripture, but God did not answer. Finally, he said to himself, "Look, I have put in this much effort, but I haven't made any progress. So I will go to see my brother and ask him."

When he had gone out, closed the door and started off, an angel of God was sent to him and said: "Seventy weeks of fasting have not brought you near to God. But now that you are humble enough to go to your brother, I have been sent to you to reveal the meanings of the words." Then the angel explained the meaning which the old man was seeking, and went away.[7]

These words, spoken almost 2000 years ago, and the stories shared in this chapter demonstrate that the way is not easy. Choosing to surrender to the mystery within our depths and trusting that the voice we hear holds a promise of new life provide the key to healing. And still we resist.

Elisabeth's Story

I remember the first time I met Elisabeth. She greeted me at the door, surrounded by the opulent furnishings of her house, with a raging headache. At the time, she was in the midst of a very significant business deal: she owed millions, and was being forced to sell off her assets. She was in court day after day, continually meeting with her lawyers and fielding questions from the media. She lived under enormous pressure, suffering daily headaches which she seemed incapable of getting rid of – even with the use of major painkillers. It seemed reasonable from my perspective to assist her in attaining temporary relief; a long-term solution was another matter. After I had worked on her for twenty minutes, her headache was gone. This began a relationship that has lasted a number of years and has prompted me to reflect on people in pain. How do they view pain? What do they need to heal? How do they deal with the vulnerability that accompanies pain?

Over time, I found that Elisabeth was a complex individual, although others did not portray her that way. As I grew to know her and watch her navigate through business deals, I became aware that she also had many serious personal challenges. As is the case in all our lives, problems, challenges and opportunities present themselves daily through our relationships with family, friends and acquaintances. On a personal level, Elisabeth was a deeply caring, compassionate woman who assisted others through very difficult circumstances. Her personal life seemed to stand in stark contrast to her public persona: the businessperson who appeared ruthless, combative, competitive and self-serving. Neither she nor the media attempted to give a more balanced view.

Elisabeth's headaches had started 20 years before, as she built her business. I sense that they relate to the fact that she never stops thinking, never stops strategizing. She seems to accept the pain as part of the price she pays for success, or success as she defines it. Although she says she'd like to be rid of pain, she has sought a solution outside herself that resides entirely in the realm of the physical. While seeking external relief, she has dipped into the spiritual world in her readings and in some of her associations but she is not yet ready to pair her spiritual curiosity and her physical condition. On one occasion, Elisabeth asked if I thought she would ever be rid of the headaches. I told her yes, but added she would need to sell all her toys and businesses and find an elder to live with in the bush. She said she could never do that!

What I meant was that until she can detach from her possessions and find solitude and peace within, Elisabeth will always battle headaches. External solutions may reduce her pain, or even cause it to abate for a time, but the real solution can only be found through a personal journey inward.

I have come to realize through my work with people who suffer that there is a place beyond pain, beyond relaxation, a place called peace. As we seek to heal, we need to visit such a place and live there as often as we can. It's a place to come to know – not intellectually, but in a sense of knowing through the whole body. In healing, we seek to find this sense of peace in each aspect, location and fibre of our lives. It is a revisiting of soul and is connected, I believe, to the divinity within us. The late poet Robert Lax speaks of the "spirit of peace within us"[8] and suggests that if we can cultivate this we are on the right track in our spiritual journey. I believe it is more than a signpost; it is an essential ingredient of our health and well-being.

To be at peace with ourselves is not reflected solely by relaxation, meditations or inactivity. It is reflected by our attitude of being, our presence regardless of the circumstances in which we find ourselves. We can be peacefully active, peacefully passionate, peacefully working, peacefully assertive and peacefully at rest. It is a way of being, not a way of doing, and can be found and held in all our daily activities and circumstances.

An integral component in healing is the ability to come to peace with our illness or injury. By embracing this aspect of ourselves and making room for it in our lives, we make it a part of who we are. We can then give some of our energy to healing. In the final analysis, we can change only that which is part of us, not that which is external. As Albert Schweitzer said, "In the end all healing is self healing." If this is true, we must own our illness/injury. Having accepted this aspect of who we are at the moment, we can peacefully move towards changing that and heal those aspects of ourselves that need healing.

In the work I've done with people who suffer without reflection and insight – unreflective warriors – I've observed that there is something very primal about our body's intuitive response to circumstances and environment. If we live in constant conflict, struggle and aggression, as Elisabeth appears to do, our bodies hold energy ready to strike out, attack, defend or take forceful action. However, the opportunity for action is often denied because we live in a world of "shoulds," where most aggressive action is discouraged. In these circumstances, the energy for transformation and healing becomes repressed and reveals itself as physical pain. What happens, I wonder, when the archetypes we live aren't made physical through our bodies? What is the personal impact of this unexpressed energy? If a warrior must restrain his or her urges, and the body mirrors life, what are the implications for health and well-being?

In becoming who we are, which Thomas Merton claimed to be the core of our spiritual journey, we must learn to deal with our hidden energies and release those energies through our physical selves. Not to do so means to live the turmoil and pain of our unawareness. As I felt the tension and pent-up energy in Elisabeth's shoulders, I commented that after fighting and arguing in court day after day, she must feel like punching someone. "I think my shoulders and back would feel a whole lot better if I could," she replied. We need to be cautious that we are releasing the energy within us, not repressing it. Peace will not be achieved by burying the hatchet but by releasing our grip on it!

Matt's Story

When Matt came to see me, he was a young, aggressive lawyer who worked 70-hour weeks and saw no other option. He travelled extensively, owned several public companies and traded in gold futures. As he drove up to our clinic and entered the building, Matt would be talking on his cell phone. Once in, he would hang up and call someone on our courtesy phone while he waited, go to the washroom and come out talking again on his cell phone. The only time he wasn't on his phone was during our session, although occasionally I agreed to let him keep the cell phone on when he had to close on a stock deal. One day he took a call during his massage, hung up and announced: "I just made $26,000!" I said, "Great! This massage just cost you a grand!"

The downside to all this work was that Matt had constant headaches, and his back hurt continually. He ate poorly, had no time for exercise and slept intermittently. He wanted me to stop the headaches and reduce his fatigue so that he could study world newspapers for longer periods, thereby improving his trading ability. In fact, he wanted to read the papers up to eight hours a day and refused to follow any treatment plan. He wondered whether I could do more for him if he paid more. While Matt was generous with money and focused with his time, he did not realize that money could not buy everything he wanted.

I worked with Matt for about three years but could not eliminate his headaches or alter his work behaviour and lifestyle. One day he called and cancelled an appointment, and I never heard from him again. I called him one day and the phone just rang and rang. There was no answering machine. He seemed to have fallen off the face of the earth.

Like many people in pain, Matt looked for a solution outside himself, but to heal he needed to go within. That requires change, and change threatened the way he chose to live at that point in time. Matt wished to remain driven, goal-oriented and focused on the desired outcome at all costs, even if it cost him his health.

Matt's situation makes me question why we put our goals above the process of attaining them. Do we need to suffer to give our goals value? Do we feel somehow that what we achieve has more worth if we have suffered for it? Is it more heroic to have endured and attained than to attain with ease? I believe that when Matt realized I could not eliminate his pain without him changing his lifestyle, he abandoned treatment. I was unable to help him, but perhaps he will find help from others or find his own way to heal.

Final Considerations

We can remain trapped within unreflective suffering – not because of the pain but because the suffering never ends. When we find ourselves in the places Elisabeth and Matt did, we never find our way through to wholeness. Just as in the Fisher King myth of the Middle Ages, the wounded king is not healed until the proper question is asked. So we never attain healing and wholeness until we surrender to the mystery of life and ask the right questions. Unfortunately, in this example, it is not just the king who suffers but also those within the kingdom who experience desolation, emptiness and unfulfillment. Thus, like the person mentioned earlier who fasted for 70 weeks, we often have to go beyond our own efforts and ask for help. No one is an island, yet we become isolated when we see ourselves as rocks, unconnected and unconnectable to God, others and the depths of our souls.

Suffering rarely occurs in isolation. It happens in community, and when our suffering lacks reflection the whole community suffers endlessly. Families, friends and associates are all affected if we fail to address our suffering to the right questions. Such questions should have the ability to lift us, and those in relationship with us, to a greater understanding of who we are. They must help us surrender to the mystery within which we live, and bring awareness of the sacred within our humanity.

Questions for Reflection

- Do I see myself in Elisabeth or Matt's story? If so, how?

- Where do I live out the patterns of being an unreflective warrior?

- Why do I do this?

- Do I value my achievements more when I have suffered for them than when they come easily?

- What do I need to shed in order to heal?

Chapter 4

Breaking Open the Husk

Truthfulness is the only currency which circulates everywhere.

— Chinese proverb

All life's battles teach us something, even those we lose. When you grow up, you'll discover that you have defended lies, deceived yourself, or suffered for foolishness. If you're a good warrior, you will not blame yourself for this, but neither will you allow your mistakes to repeat themselves.

— Paulo Coelho

Authenticity and integrity or inner harmony are related to the choices made on the basis of who we are and what we love.

— Jean S. Bolen, MD

What happens when the husk around us breaks open? In the literature of the sacred, the breaking of the husk around the core of being represents movement towards healing and wholeness. What does it take for a person's husk to be opened, and that person transformed? The husk represents the various walls, shields, barriers and stories we use to shield us from the deepest parts of our souls.

Over a period of years, I watched the unfolding of a friend's life. Unreflectiveness dominated his life, yet he wanted to be a healer. As a healer he was kind, compassionate and caring towards his students and those who sought him for counselling. Yet he could not be so charitable with himself. There were many unrealistic expectations, some inherited from family and society and some erected to guard his deepest self. These put him into deeper and deeper depression and physical disarray. While my friend could ask his clients and students to care for themselves, taking time to rest, reflect and sort through their priorities, his inner warrior demanded more and more of his own "noble" energy to save everyone around him. The struggle between the demons of perfection and nobility and his desire to be compassionate and caring almost destroyed him. No medication, holiday or change of scenery could bring a sense of meaning and joy to his life. Instead, the poisonous useless stories dominated his life and almost brought about his demise.

The husk, or protective coat, had to break open before healing could begin. Denial, blaming others, wanting to circumvent the process and anger fought against his innate desire to be whole. Yet, at the core of his being, he knew the path he had to take.

The husk that protects us from the "gold" within opens gingerly – and ever so slowly. Some writers maintain that only great pain or joy frees us to reach into our depths in this way. They might be right. Both pain and joy can break boundaries and walls to reveal energies and resources we never realized we possessed. Usually, trauma or great love frees people to be who they are called to be.

Over the years, we have all met people who have healed in one way or another. It might be the person living with AIDS who has overcome bitterness at being rejected by family, friends or peers when he revealed his sexual orientation or illness. Or it could have been the person who found herself in a destructive relationship, whether it was with a spouse, parent, friend, colleague or neighbour. In each case, they reached deep inside to discover their whole. Yet the struggle to fight destructive patterns of thoughts, actions or relationships demands the energy of a warrior who believes in a cause and is willing to fight for it.

People come in many shapes and colours, but all possess a courageous warrior ready to struggle for what they believe is right and good. For many, the warrior has often been strangled, neglected or diminished within, yet for healing and transformation to occur the warrior needs to awaken and help the person find new life. Healing is brought about through therapy, support groups, prayer, spiritual direction, retreats and solitude or through friendship and rediscovery of one's inner worth and beauty. We wrestle along the way with hostility towards those who have hurt us, and with self-rejection.

Whether one struggles with disappointment, deep-seated hostility, cancer, financial failure, fear of rejection and abandonment or asks "Why me?" strength of mind lights the way through the darkness and on the path to healing. Determined courage, filled with hope of transformation, awakens our deepest feelings of self-worth and dignity. Thus, the sacred is roused within and releases the power of grace to help us through. Sometimes we fight alone, at other times we have someone with us. While we may sometimes want the companionship of like-minded people to help us through, there are occasions when we are personally put to the test. It's during these moments that we either find the inner courage and grace to move on or succumb once again to despair, self-disregard, paralysis and self-destruction.

I recently heard two stories of personal transformation that occurred at a continuing care centre when birds and other pets were introduced onto the nursing units. In one unit, where the residents were alert and somewhat mobile, someone brought in a bird. Suddenly, people who had not left their rooms except for meals started to congregate near the bird and talk to one another. Unfortunately, when a window was left open and the room became cold, the bird developed pneumonia and eventually died. With its death, people returned to their own rooms and separate worlds.

However, a nurse who had noticed the change in behaviour decided to bring her own three birds into the care centre for the residents. She created a special space for the birds with soft music in the background, and people came out of their rooms once again. People who had not talked in a long time began to communicate. The same healing occurred when a person who had no desire to talk with people was "adopted" by a cat that moved onto a unit. The cat decided to make this person his friend, and suddenly a person who had turned into himself broke open and reconnected with family, staff and the people around him.

As mentioned previously, during the early years of Christianity, men and women moved to the margins of society in the deserts of Egypt and the Middle East; they also moved into the caves and rugged terrain of western Ireland. The migration happened so that people could grapple with their personal demons and know themselves, others, God and Creation in a deeper, authentic way. Throughout history, the human struggle with inner demons had been a central theme, with the slow, painful surrender to grace and courage that concludes in transformation. Remember the story of Jacob, shared in the book of Genesis.

> Jacob was left alone. And there was one who wrestled with him until daybreak who, seeing that he could not master him, struck him in the socket of his hip, and Jacob's hip was dislocated as he wrestled with him. He said, "Let me go, for day is breaking." But Jacob answered, "I will not let you go unless you bless me." He then asked, "What is your name?" "Jacob," he replied. He said, "Your name shall no longer be Jacob, but Israel, because you have been strong against God, and you shall prevail against men." ...Jacob named the place Peniel, "Because I have seen God face to face...and survived." (Genesis 32:24-32)

For Jacob, and in fact all of us, this struggle demands a singleness of purpose, a sense that we are doing the right thing and a willingness to risk. Without these, we stumble and find ourselves stuck inside our pain and ruled by our demons.

One final example may help to clarify the point. Once, I was talking to a physician about the process of soul-healing as people died. He had an elderly female patient who had suffered a great deal of anguish and was dying; nothing could help her. Finally someone asked her what it was she could not abandon, so that she could die peacefully. At the core of it was her closely held belief that her daughter had hated her for the last 40 years, because she had denied her ballet lessons as a young child. The daughter was called and travelled from a distant location to tell her mother, "No, I have not disliked you for all these years. I understood there was no money during that time for the lessons. And I always knew you loved me." For 40 years, the woman had seen everything through that lens of presumed failure, but when she found the courage to confront her demon of presumed failure she was finally free to find healing and peace in the last days of her life.

It is to be hoped that the warrior's spirit emerges several times in life, not just at its end. When this happens, healing flows from both the inward and outward journeys. For many, the experience demands attention to dreams, where we often find hints of healing. By befriending the dream, writing it down or sharing it with a friend, we respect it. And by respecting it, a pathway to healing begins to emerge. Over the years, I have been amazed how dreams have paved the way for new life, both for myself and others. Decisions and choices have been made, courage found, challenges issued and comfort dispersed based upon the assertive power of my dreams. While being attentive to dreams is not the only way the husk opens and we find the strength to heal, it is one means. Keeping a journal, drawing, dance, writing, poetry, photography, pottery and a variety of other creative endeavours, coupled with solitude and meditation, may help.

While an unreflective person may consider the phrase "no pain, no gain" as a justification for persisting in suffering, as the husk opens and he or she surrenders to the mystery, it becomes obvious that it is only through pain befriended and transformed that healing and wholeness occur. While the journey is not always easy, it is significant.

Doug's Story

Doug had been searching for the body of his ten-year-old son in a creek close to my office for about a week before I realized I knew Doug and his family. During spring thaw, his son had been playing inside a culvert when he slipped into the water, drowned and was swept under the ice. Community members soon joined in searching for the boy, as Doug could not rest until his son's body was recovered. The city police had tried to stop him and the local community members in their search, yet they persisted. The ice was dangerous, the temperature well below zero. City officials wanted Doug and the others to wait several months for a full thaw to produce his child's body, but Doug desperately wanted his son's body found.

I felt I needed to help Doug personally, so I went to the creek to offer the one thing I could best contribute – a massage. At that point, Doug had slept only a few hours in the past week. He had been searching day and night and I knew that he must be sore. If he insisted on continuing, I thought maybe I could help his body stay strong. It was another five days before my offer was accepted. Doug's brother phoned midday and asked if I could work on Doug that evening, as he was extremely sore and fatigued from so many days of standing in the frigid water. We arranged for Doug to be brought to my office at 10:30 that night.

I worked with Doug for more than an hour. As I worked we spoke about the hope and possibility that he might find his son the next day. We both felt quite confident about that, and the energy in the room took on the feeling of preparing a warrior for his greatest challenge. The session's intent became one of preparation and readiness instead of rest and recovery. Doug's body felt strong and confident underneath the fatigue. When his brother returned to pick him up, Doug went home to catch seven hours of sleep, the most he had had in two weeks.

On my way to work the next day, something told me to forget all else and find Doug. I drove to the creek, parked my truck close to the bridge where Doug's son had fallen and began running downstream. As I arrived at the side of the creek where Doug stood, he reached under the ice and shouted, "I found him!" He then carefully lifted the body of his son to the edge of the creek. Just as strongly as I had felt called to find Doug, I now felt compelled to leave him with his family and friends to grieve. I felt no need to remain with them, and certainly no need to watch their grief. I silently thanked God, turned and walked away.

We all are called upon to overcome obstacles at different times, and for different reasons. When we're wounded, the opportunity exists for a warrior to arise in our being, and we are given the chance to grow spiritually. This requires that we let down the mask, break open the husk, if only for a short time, and share our pain and vulnerability with another. On an unconscious level, we know what we need. Having the courage to do as Doug did, not only to fight the fight but to reach out for support, enables us to continue the journey. Doug knew what he needed in order to heal and move on with his life. He also knew he needed the support of others, so he reached out and embraced the help offered. Doug shared his grief, pain and vulnerability. The husk around his life broke open publicly, and when it did he was single-minded in his desire to heal, despite the risks. Like Doug, we too must ask for what we need, so that we can find our way through our anguish.

Brent's Story

For years, there were two things that drove Brent: his twin desires to rescue others from their problems and to build a successful consulting business. These motivations appeared to work well: he became a highly successful consultant, sought after throughout North America. Unfortunately, they also proved to be his downfall.

Brent often worked 80-hour weeks, paying little attention to anything except the project at hand. He generally worked alone, although at one point he hired another consultant; it seemed like a good time to expand. The business grew and goals were consistently met, but the financial rewards ebbed and flowed and it never really flourished.

Brent's personal life was also affected by his need to rescue others. He was surrounded by many people with both personal and professional problems whom he unselfishly assisted. Brent was most compassionate, and many people drew on his advice and assistance. This meant that, often, when he wasn't solving people's business woes he was trying to resolve their personal problems.

After a number of years, the consultant he had hired to work with him left the job because she recognized, with Brent's assistance, that she was not truly happy. The intensity of this type of work deprived her of any outside life. Following her departure, Brent just picked up her remaining responsibilities, in addition to the work he was already doing, and pressed on. Now he was never home, always working and becoming increasingly exhausted. After a year or two, his life crashed. A longstanding personal relationship ended, he was unable to focus and in the end stopped working for about two years.

This crisis in Brent's life gave him the time he needed to reflect. With the assistance of a therapist, Brent began to sort out the motivations that drove him, where they originated and how they affected his life. He began to know himself, possibly for the first time.

As it often does, it took a crisis for Brent to move from unreflective suffering to healing. Without a certain amount of suffering, we seem to persist in the patterns that got us where we are. When the husk broke around Brent's life, as painful as it was for him and those closest to him, he was finally able to reach inward to find understanding, meaning and answers. He came to understand the expectations that he had subconsciously inherited from his family, how they played out in his life and served him, both positively and negatively. He began to know another part of himself, to mine the gold within, and find the strength to recognize when he was slipping into destructive patterns.

Brent has now returned to work, which he does well in a healthy manner by limiting the time he spends working, taking less ownership for finding solutions to other people's problems and choosing his work and relationships carefully. His clients never deserted him, his close friendships remain and the intimacy he has in his relationships is genuine and healthy. Brent enjoys life much more now. He laughs more often, and takes pleasure in building a way of life that supports who he wants to be.

Brent must remain vigilant about slipping into old patterns, because his inherited ways and perceptions will likely remain with him; they just won't run his life. A monk at the Camoldali Hermitage in Big Sur, California, once told me: "Our issues will always be with us; we must make them our friends, because each time they arise they give us the opportunity to learn something new, something deeper about ourselves. It's in staying vigilant that we come to know who we are."

The unaware life is not free. Without knowing ourselves well and constantly observing ourselves, as a scientist might observe an anthill, we are captive to the unconscious, inherent attachments that dictate our lives. We don't know why we do what we do, and why we do not take other actions. If we stay unaware of the underlying motivations, fears and affiliations in our lives, then our reactions are not freely chosen and often reflect parental or societal responses.

Until Brent was in crisis, he could not see how his inherent motivations and attachments dictated his choices. He thought he was doing as he pleased, when in fact he was doing what he had always done. Now, after a time of healing, he sees his choices from outside of his attachments, carefully weighing motivations and always remaining wary for when they might sneak up and snatch his freedom away. Brent learned a lesson that can help us all: to be aware and vigilant, objectively watching ourselves and recognizing that we are more – and other – than our reactions to our environment. I am reminded of the insight of a twelfth-century writer, Juan Ramon Jimenez, who stated:

> I am not I. I am the one walking beside me, whom I do not see, whom at times I manage to visit, and whom at other times I forget, who remains calm and silent while I talk, and forgives gently when I hate, who walks where I am not, who will remain standing when I die.[9]

Final Considerations

The courage needed to wrestle with our inner demons as Jacob did in the Scriptures, and as all of us do in our private lives, lies at the core of who we are. Over and over, we need to let go of the idols, images, stories, actions and ways of seeing things that no longer give us life. In doing so, we must bravely trek through the darkness at the depths of our souls in order to find new life.

The life experiences of both Doug and Brent also reveal the power of asking for help in the midst of suffering. The way to healing comes when we surrender our need to do it all. It is then that the husk opens.

Questions for Reflection

- How do I open myself to the sacred and gold within?

- What barriers exist to my healing and growth?

- How and when do I live the warrior image in terms of my own healing and growth?

- What demons have I had to wrestle with?

- What is an important lesson for me from this section?

Chapter 5

The Pain Beneath the Pain

Soul pain is the experience of an individual who has
become disconnected and alienated from the deepest and
most fundamental aspects of himself or herself.
— *Michael Kearney, MD*

In the middle of difficulty lies opportunity.
— *Albert Einstein*

One day, a physician described to me a tense moment
with a patient in her final days of life. While the
woman had sufficient medication to ease the physical
pain, her soul pain could not be soothed. She said, in
her native tongue, that all she could feel was "*agonia.*" I
have never forgotten the phrase, for it captured instantly
the experience of "pain beneath the pain." What lurked
beneath this woman's physical pain I do not know, yet
each of us carries unresolved pain within us. The
physician, a specialist in palliative care, recognized the
pain for what it was and could only offer the comfort of
listening to her unresolved life story. While the woman's
soul pain was not resolved before her death, she did
experience the compassionate listening of her physician

– something that had evidently been missing for far too long in her life.

It is often hard to grow in consciousness and let go of images, stories and experiences that no longer have meaning. A broken relationship or a dream not pursued may cause pain that lingers deep within. I remember being at a dinner party in a restaurant when one of the guests invited each of us to reveal what we would be doing if we could do just as we liked. Interestingly, most of us identified something other than what we were presently doing. What does that say about our lives? I fear it reveals that we may have chosen more practical roles in life than what dwells in our souls. What happens, then, to that dream over a lifetime? Does it remain unattended? Do we grow bitter with regret and disappointment that we never fulfilled it? Our bodies and souls do not lie, and when we neglect what they say to us we do so at our peril!

I often ask people who work in continuing care facilities what they learn from the people entrusted to their care during the final months or years of these clients' lives. They frequently tell me they see the type of person they would like to become in their final years – or the opposite. Most of us want to become people who are happy and engaged, not snarled in bitterness, regret and disillusionment. Yet when these same caregivers are asked how they are conducting their lives to ensure this does not occur, they often look dumbfounded. We do not always know how to make the choices that will enable us to move through unresolved life issues. Instead, we often approach life as if we expect some kind of magic to bring resolution.

In a spirituality class I once taught, one of my students was a recreational therapist who worked in a chronic care facility. I asked, "Just what do you do as a recreational therapist in such a setting?" Basically, she said, "I help people to make sense of their lives." When I asked how, she replied that "people are full of hurts, fears and issues that still linger within and seek meaning." She said that through the interaction with others that she provides, unresolved areas of life emerge and seek expression.

In classical Christian spirituality, the "dark night of the soul" represents a movement through darkness and the peeling away of images, stories, experiences and events that no longer sustain or hold us hostage. Safe passage demands courage, support and a belief that one will come through it with a renewed sense of hope and a healing of what has kept us stuck. As many writers in classical Christian spirituality attest, the dark night is about encountering the love of the sacred in new and profound ways. It's also about shedding magical images of God and ourselves. It's a stripping away of what has propped us up, so that we can move into a more authentic expression of life. This is vividly portrayed in Dante's *Divine Comedy* as he weaves his way through hell and purgatory, escorted by the Roman poet Virgil and guided through heaven by his former lover Beatrice. In Dante's work, we see portrayed the struggle to find meaning in life. There is the descent into the pits of hell, where darkness, suffering and, finally, ice hold people captive. In purgatory people are waiting their admission into heaven, but are not quite ready to go. This is not unlike us: we cannot rush our way through the "dark night."

There are no easy steps. Instead, we have to move at a rhythm that may be quite foreign to us. Finally, a breakthrough occurs; we experience a new sense of purpose, meaning and light in life.

When we have pain living deep inside us, it demands attention. If we believe that mind, body and soul form an integrated whole, then we cannot separate one part from the other. Yet we often try to do so. In fact, the Western medical model usually looks only at a presenting ailment and does not seek to understand the whole picture. We are often more keen to seek a quick fix rather than to go into the suffering to see what message awaits.

A number of years ago, I experienced great discomfort in one of my kidneys. After various consults and discussions of possible causes, I told my physician that before undergoing any more tests I wanted to explore something else. I recalled that kidneys purify the contents of our bodies, and realized that I had started a new spiritual counselling practice without allowing sufficient time between clients. Instead of discovering my own rhythm, I had followed the example of others whom I deeply admired and booked back-to-back meetings with clients for counselling. While back-to-back meetings work for some, for me it proved disastrous. What I needed was a break between clients so I could process what I had heard. When I made the connection and changed my timetable, the physical symptoms of kidney trouble disappeared. I returned to my physician and explained that the issue was how I was living my life; the kidney tension had revealed a deeper source of discomfort.

In the midst of pain we are challenged to ask, "Where is the sacred? What grace lies deep inside of me that I have yet to experience and integrate into my life?" How we answer these questions reveals how we integrate spirituality and healing amid pain so deep we often cannot find words or images to describe it or trace its root cause. Spirituality brings depth into the centre of our life and sheds the facades, easy answers and facile remedies. It demands patience and a willingness to live with mystery and hear what lies beyond the physical manifestations of our bodies.

Betty's Story

Betty's physician referred her to me after six months of intensive physical therapy had failed to reduce the pain in her shoulder. She had been injured while skiing during the previous Christmas vacation, and my physical examination revealed a great deal of muscle tension throughout her shoulder and neck region, as if the shoulders were locked down on the torso.

Over a period of time, Betty began to relax and became increasingly aware of her body and pain during our sessions. One day as I worked on her shoulder she began to cry. Her tears were the beginning of her healing, although Betty initially had a difficult time determining why she was crying. Soon, however, it became evident that she was remembering her son's death that had taken place just before Christmas the year before her skiing accident. Betty's son had committed suicide; the family had taken the ski vacation a year after his death to try and move on from the experience. Betty indicated that she had grieved for her son's death for awhile then decided it was time to stop and grieve no more. She never cried about it again until our session.

It seems to me that although Betty had intellectually decided that she was through grieving, her body and her unconscious mind had not reached closure. Her "accident" and subsequent pain triggered a return to the deeper pain she still retained. As she returned to grieving for her son's death, the pain in her shoulder decreased, her mobility increased and the neck and shoulder began to heal. Betty began seeing a psychologist, something she had not done before, to help her work through her son's death while she continued with massage therapy.

Betty's experience demonstrates for me the relationship between healing and our spiritual journey. It shows that the intention to return to wholeness, as shown by Betty's persistence in undertaking both physical and massage therapy, is not enough. That intention needs to be coupled with awareness to truly achieve healing. Had Betty not been able to recognize that her "accidental" injury and pain were connected in some way to her need to complete the grieving process, I do not believe her shoulder would have recovered. She might have carried the unresolved pain until such time as she healed from the death of her son. By dealing only ~~~~ the physical pain, she was able to avoid the real ~~~~f over the loss of her son. In my view, if ~~~~pists deal only with the physical ~~~~s of our clients' pain, we are actually enabling them to stay in pain and, in fact, are becoming codependent with the client.

Intention alone is like water pressure in a hose that no one is holding: the water is running out, but without someone's awareness to direct its pressure, little is accomplished. On the other hand, awareness without intent also accomplishes little, because it is the pressure and focus of intent that moves an individual to act. True, sustainable healing requires both intention and awareness. Often it is the pain we suffer that provides the stimulus required to form our intent to heal. The necessary awareness can be nurtured from continually searching within our own experience for deeper meaning. With the marriage of these two factors, we can heal.

Betty needed to be treated as a whole person, to allow all of her experience to be brought into the healing process. To deal with her pain only as a physical outcome of injury was incomplete. Her pain ought to be seen as a manifestation of a deeper, more spiritual pain. Her body sought to reunite her as a whole person, which required her to seek counselling for her emotional pain while continuing to receive treatment for the physical symptoms of that pain.

To refer the client to psychological or spiritual counselling and abandon physical therapy is not useful because it ignores the reality of the individual's physical pain and the pathway the body presents for healing the whole person. To do one without the other would be less than effective.

This moment in the therapeutic process can be extremely delicate. It is a point during which the client's perspective and expectations may collide with the therapist's experience concerning what needs to be done to facilitate healing. Clients may not be ready to explore the underlying dimensions of their pain, regardless of how effective that may be. They may seek to avoid the inner work necessary to truly heal; indeed, some may be in their current situation because they avoid inner work.

It is important to remember, at this stage, who is who. It's important to respect the client's process or journey and begin where he or she is. While therapists should raise the possible benefits to exploring the "pain beneath the pain" and offer options for doing so, in the end the client's decision to proceed or not proceed must be respected. Patience, support and encouragement are vital in caring for the client throughout this process. This is no time for therapeutic ego. It is the client's life, the sufferer's journey, and others have no right to force the process.

The same holds true whether the individual is a client, a friend in need, a spouse or a family member. The individual who holds the pain also holds the responsibility for moving towards healing. It is his or her journey; how he or she chooses to heal is a personal choice. We can be present to encourage, point the way or just hold a space for their healing, but we cannot force the process. There is nothing to be gained in pushing the river.

Paula's Story

Paula was referred to me by her personal trainer. She was in her mid-60s, had recently married a widower and was experiencing pain in her upper arm. Her trainer thought this was due to muscle tension, but when I began working with her I assessed that the pain was referred from trigger points in the anterior neck region. In addition, she began to experience pain in her hips and leg that she thought might be due to walking or sitting on a too-soft couch. Her pain improved following each of our weekly sessions but soon returned, her body demonstrating that she needed to stay in control. During the sessions we would observe her physical state, prompting her to reflect that she always felt on guard and tended to raise her shoulders and pull in her head as if she could withdraw into her shell. Her mid-back and shoulders were continually tense, and she became increasingly aware of when she would "turn into a turtle" during the day.

With this increased awareness, she began to observe her life and reflect on it. She wondered why her body didn't feel like she controlled it anymore, and shared with me that she had only recently remarried. Her first husband had been deceased for many years. She noticed that her physical condition began to change after she moved into her new husband's home, which had been decorated and furnished by his late spouse. She felt relaxed and at ease when visiting her lake cottage but observed that as she drove to her new home after time at the cottage, the pain in her legs and shoulders arose. She also noticed that she felt increasingly uncomfortable with the photographs of their respective deceased spouses, and the fresh flowers that they kept beside the photos.

Paula's realizations distressed her, but also showed her a way out of her pain. In coming to this understanding, Paula began to take charge of her life and found it increasingly easy to release the muscular tension in her body. She had fewer episodes of pain in her shoulders and legs. Paula decided that she needed to remove the old photos and clear the energy of her husband's deceased wife from the house and furnishings. She determined that she would write a letter to her husband's deceased wife, read the letter and then burn it and clear the deceased woman's energy from the house by smudging her home with traditional Native sweet grass. Although she did not actually undertake this whole ritual, she was able to let go of the tension and subsequent pain just through the realization of the cause.

Paula's experience demonstrates for me the impact of environment on our bodies. It also shows the extent to which our bodies mirror what's going on in our internal world and how that is affected by our environment. Further, her experience shows that when we are not aware of what is affecting us we feel out of control, attacked and defensive. As we become conscious of the factors affecting us, we are able to let down our defences, recover our true selves and re-establish health.

Final Considerations

In each of these stories, soul pain as it is described by Michael Kearney, MD, revealed itself through physical symptoms. Often hidden and disguised, soul pain pushes us deeper into our very being and demands surrender to a power and insight much larger than ourselves. Like the woman in the Scriptures who had been "suffering from a hemorrhage for twelve years, whom no one had been able to cure," (Luke 8:43) we too find ourselves often suffering. And like her, we often need to go deeper into the mystery of life to experience healing. As Jesus might say to any one of us, "your faith has restored you to health." (Luke 8:48)

Without going deeper, many people remain trapped in unnecessary suffering from regret, avoidance, denial and unawareness. We often feel like Jesus did on the cross when he cried out, "My God, my God, why have you deserted me?" (Mark 15:34) Yet, like Jesus, we can also say: "Father, into your hands I commit my spirit." (Luke 23:46) As Einstein's quote at the beginning of this chapter declares, it is up to us – and our guides – to steadfastly wait for the opportunity to break through and recognize it when it comes.

Many people choose to delay deeper introspection, hoping the crisis will pass or that they can somehow work their way through without delving into their own unknown. The "dark night of the soul" is not a place one enters eagerly. Few of us rise each morning ready to dig up our inadequacies, mull over character flaws, review resentments or work on spiritual failings that have the potential to impede our ability to heal. Generally, we must be in considerable pain and suffering to motivate such introspection.

However, we should embark on just such an undertaking. Each and every day we need time to reflect on the successes and failures we encountered, reconcile ourselves with the reality we lived that day and learn, let go and move on. Bringing this level of awareness to our day-to-day existence provides the potential to relieve suffering, lighten the path and, with any luck, speed the dawn after any dark night we may suffer.

Questions for Reflection

- How does soul pain reveal itself in my life through physiological and psychological symptoms?

- With whose story in this chapter do I relate more? Why?

- Who and what drain my energy and hope for the future?

- What are the hidden images, stories and experiences that may cause pain in my life?

- How comfortable am I in learning to go through the inner darkness that often surrounds my life experience?

- How do forgiveness and reconciliation enter into my healing process?

Chapter 6

The Quest for Congruency

Live in the open.

— Auguste Comte

I am finally coming out of a chrysalis. The years behind
me seem strangely inert and negative, but I suppose that
passivity was necessary. Now the pain and struggle of
fighting my way out into something new and much bigger.
I must see and embrace God in the whole world.

— Thomas Merton

As we grow older, we become kinder; there is no mistake
which I have not already made.

— Goethe

Not long ago I visited a friend who had just finished
a sabbatical, and was struck by the sense of peace,
meaning and purpose that shaped her life. In fact, she
reminded me of just how unbalanced and incongruent I
was at times. Somewhere over the years, the various
aspects of body, mind and soul had come together so
well for her that both I and another friend of mine
remarked, "Wow, she is one together woman!" Rarely
do we come into contact with a person so well integrated

whose very presence challenges us to go deeper and explore our own lives.

As I reflect upon this meeting, I am continually challenged to think about my life and how I'm living it. How do I embrace those aspects of my life that give it real meaning and dignity, and how do I shed those activities, attitudes and behaviours that diminish and decimate my life? The journey towards congruence asks those types of questions.

Maybe no other part of our journey demands such brutal honesty with ourselves in terms of how we live and honour mind, body and soul. These three aspects of life demand equal attention. There are times when we focus on one over the other, but there are also times when we resist bringing the truth of who we are into relationships with self, others and all Creation. Each of us knows how easy it is to betray ourselves. The question becomes this: Has our betrayal of deepest self become a way of life? Have we lost touch with our essence as someone who is loved and immersed in the power of a living God no matter how much we forget, turn away or reject God's invitation to meet the sacred in all aspects of life?

The invitation to be congruent scares us, because it means part of the persona and way of life we have developed to protect ourselves from the urgings of soul needs to be shed. As the Merton quote that begins this chapter suggests, suddenly we find ourselves breaking out of our cocoon of inertia and passivity and being invited to embrace a larger image of God, Creation and self. And, like Merton, we need to fight our way out of patterns that no longer honour who we really are. The patterns can refer to something as simple as the types of food we eat, how we spend our time and with whom, or styles of relationships with self, others, work and environment that no longer nurture our lives. The task is not simple. A quote in German that I came across captures the tension as we try to move beyond inertia and struggle free of inner and outer constraints: "*Ich stehe mir im Weg*" – I am standing in my own way.

Each of us needs to discover: How am I standing in my own way? Is it because I fear or dislike my core being? Because I do not have a desire to grow? I remember a friend of mine, concerned about her weight, who had a picture of a grossly overweight person on her refrigerator. The picture revealed one of her deepest fears – that she would let herself go or eat away her frustrations. Both were potential patterns that needed to be broken for her to become more congruent. Yet the struggle to reject eating as a way to numb the inner longings of the soul and ease the frustration of broken dreams reveals just part of the effort to find a new relationship within mind, body and soul.

We need to make a total commitment to becoming congruent. Such a commitment calls for physical, mental and spiritual wellness. If one of these elements is lacking, underdeveloped or ignored, we falter. Think of the three-legged stool. We all know what happens when one or more of the legs becomes weak or breaks: the stool tumbles over, taking us with it. By the same token, if we neglect our soul work, do not listen to our dreams and fail to make some quiet in our life to nurture those elements of our being that cry out for mystery and beauty, we suffer. No matter how strong we are or how well our mind works, a constituent ingredient to who we are as people is missing and the sought after harmony disappears.

In seeking congruence, we commit ourselves to a healthy way of living that has meaning. Too often, happiness remains elusive. I believe we really want a life filled with meaning and purpose, grounded in meaning and providing depth for ourselves and those around us. A meaningful life provides the inner framework to help us move through suffering as well as joy, and to discover grace in good times and bad times. Within this context, we become more of who we are because we abandon everything that is not us: expectations of self and others, beliefs as well as actions, attitudes and values that no longer have substance.

Striving for a congruent and integrated life demands a willingness to know ourselves well, and humility, the ability to be neither more nor less than we were created to be, guides the unfolding process. Humility requires that we develop those gifts dormant within ourselves. I was talking with a friend recently about when he was going to resume drawing or painting. "Later," he said. Yet I wonder if some of his angst flows from the fact that there is a part of himself that longs to be expressed but isn't, because of commitments to a young family and a very demanding job. I also wonder if the stomach acid, the twitching eye and the push for success would not be mellowed if he made time to pick up the pencils and chalks to draw again. Artistic pursuits invite the inner self to emerge, and a very creative part of the soul releases itself into the larger arena.

Humility also demands that we recognize our limits. We would benefit from asking ourselves: What can I do and do well? One day I asked an acquaintance, after his workout, "How are you?" He said, "I worked out so hard I almost vomited!" Taken aback, I asked, "Where is the balance?" "There is none!" he said. Honest words, but painful consequences. The same can be said for people who feel that they must always be available. Where is the time for ourselves? Do we always need to be in easy reach? Often as I sit waiting for a plane to depart, I see people frantically rushing to make just one more phone call. And of course, as we walk off the plane the cell phones go on and people begin to talk again. Is all this contact important, or is it only a way to fill the longing within our souls for something deeper? The great Russian writer Leo Tolstoy said, "The humbler a person is, the freer and stronger he is."[10] Yet, to reach that moment of integrated insight demands for many of us a re-evaluation of who we are and what gives meaning and dignity to our lives.

Humility – knowing our strengths and weaknesses; being willing to attend to our mind, body and soul in a consistent manner – paves the way to a life congruent in nature. As the following story from a Desert Father reveals, humility and inner integrity demand self-knowledge.

Abba Xanthias said, "A dog is better than I am because a dog also has love but, unlike I myself, the dog does not pass judgement."

Abba Sarmatas said, "I prefer a person who has sinned if he knows that he sinned and has repented, over a person who has not sinned and considers himself to be righteous."[11]

The choice for authenticity demands the courage to act upon our convictions. Insight and words do not suffice. Too often, we fall prey to seeking the path of least resistance, but in so doing we miss the beauty of our true nature and the gift of ourselves that we bring to family, friends, colleagues, society and God.

Rachel's Story

Rachel walked into the reception area, took one look at me and started crying. She handed me a two-page list of her physical ailments and we proceeded upstairs to my treatment room. It was obvious that Rachel was in pain. We needed to discover what contributed most to her pain, and what we should do to help her deal with it.

As Rachel began to give me her most recent history, it became apparent that the numerous deaths of family members that she had experienced over a relatively short period of time were overwhelming her. These deaths seemed to cause a crisis for Rachel, bringing up many old memories for her. Her pain had become intolerable.

On a weekly basis over the next four years, Rachel recounted many of the physical, emotional and spiritual injuries and abuses that she had suffered. Many of these wounds were debilitating, involving physical and emotional abuses as a young child; betrayals within her closest relationships; prolonged separation from her children while she was in a sanitorium being treated for tuberculosis, the removal of a lung and seven ribs; the breakdown of silicone breast implants following her lung surgery; and the death of a daughter, grandson, her parents and all her siblings. It seemed to me that any one of these issues would be enough for a lifetime! I find it amazing that she has continued to work through it all. What I find most fascinating about Rachel's story, however, is her enduring search for wholeness. She is steadfastly determined to bring together mind, body and soul as a congruent, interrelated unit.

In listening to Rachel's story, I was struck by how she continually sought to understand the purpose of her experiences, the reason beyond the obvious and what she was to learn from all this. She has used many approaches to seek out and understand her circumstances, including past life regressions, shamanistic journeys and psychic experiences, in addition to psychotherapy, Christian prayer, meditation and church attendance. All these experiences have one commonality: they sought to lead Rachel to greater self-knowledge, a sense of wholeness and congruency.

Rachel's pain remains, but it does not occupy as large a part of her life as it once did. As she comes to terms with her history and increases awareness of her life within a larger context, she puts her pain in perspective. She seems able to experience pain and reflect on it, but not be overwhelmed by it. She is not cured of her pain, and may never be, but it has its place in her life. She has healed a great deal and continues to grow in her healing each day. Rachel is truly a model of the quest for congruency that is implicit in the healing journey.

Rachel teaches us that the desire to heal our wounds is strong and enduring, and that the search for wholeness can take many forms. Some of these approaches result in apparent dead ends, but the effort is not futile. Some approaches to understanding ourselves and our experiences bear fruit, others do not. While our journey may appear to others to be eccentric, repetitive, boring, fascinating or just plain "out there," we must persevere as long as it is leading us to wholeness and healing. We cannot predetermine or anticipate on which path we will find truth. As Robert Frost wrote in his famous poem, "The Road Not Taken,"

> Two roads diverged in a wood and I –
> I took the one less traveled by,
> And that has made all the difference.[12]

Kim's Story

Kim came to see me a number of years ago. She was young, pretty and talented, with a promising opera career ahead of her. She also had a sore neck that she thought was affecting her ability to sing. Kim was one of the lead sopranos in an opera that was passing through town and needed her voice to be in top form. As I worked with her, we came to realize that her pain was originating in her chest, not her neck. She recognized that she had difficulty taking a full breath and that her voice didn't seem her own anymore. Although she had told no one in her industry, she was frightened that she was losing her voice and that her career would be finished.

Without connecting her current situation to the past, Kim told me that several months earlier a relationship in which she was heavily engaged had ended because her feelings were not returned. She had been hurt by this breakup and had consciously chosen to protect her heart from any further pain that might stem from romantic relationships. As she told her story, it became apparent that when she decided to close herself off, her body became hypertense throughout the chest and neck region. Without knowing it she had encapsulated her heart in a hypertense torso, thereby restricting her breathing as well as her ability to express her voice.

During our subsequent sessions Kim decided she needed to open up again, that in protecting her heart she had unknowingly caused her current problem. It became clear to her that protecting herself in this manner demanded too great a price. Kim was able to connect with the injured part of herself, and began to understand how the circumstances of her life were reflected in her body. This realization moved her towards healing in only a few massage sessions which focused on opening her chest to eliminate the original neck pain, re-establish her breathing and return her sense of having her own voice.

This story demonstrates the significant unconscious relationship between life experiences and the physical body. It shows that our bodies mirror life in an attempt to hold one congruent story together within the core of our being. Our bodies know our true intentions and attempt to reflect the meaning we give to our experiences. If our experience is one of pain from which we seek to withdraw, our body will try to accommodate, creating physical barriers wherever possible between us and the pain we seek to avoid. If our intent is to open up to life, recapture our vulnerability, surrender to our experiences and release our sense of control, our bodies will respond by relaxing, becoming supple and releasing the pain we hold within ourselves.

We must be continually watchful of our true intent, however. While we may say we desire one thing, our thoughts, choices and actions often reveal that we want something else. While we believe that we wish to live pain-free, we sometimes continue to hold onto practices that advance our pain. While we desire to be open, honest and vulnerable, we may hold back in certain areas we are not yet ready to expose. Without this congruency our bodies do not completely respond, as they must hold that part of being within an integrated physical presence. But the part of ourselves that we hold back may be one of the key elements to true healing. We cannot completely heal if we are withholding some portion of our experience from the process of attaining an integrated, congruent self.

Final Considerations

The quest for congruency demands attention to who we are, what motivates us and how what we do mirrors the core of our lives. The journey inward is often not easy, especially if we encounter neglected or rejected parts of our self. Yet it is the embracing of all these parts that allows the true self to emerge. In the Scriptures, the story of the Samaritan woman who encounters Jesus at the well reveals the essence of congruency. When Jesus tells her to "go and call your husband," she replies that she has no husband. Jesus responds, "You are right to say 'I have no husband'; for although you have had five, the one you have now is not your husband. You spoke the truth there." (John 4:16-18) As we become more congruent, more willing to speak the truth to ourselves, others and God, we become healing presences for ourselves and the world around us. As the Desert Father Isidore of Pelusia said,

> Living without speaking is better than speaking without living. For a person who lives rightly helps us by silence, while one who talks too much annoys us. If, however, words and life go hand in hand, it is the perfection of all philosophy.[13]

Questions for Reflection

- What aspects of these stories resonate with my own life story?

- What is my soul asking of me right now? Am I willing to listen and respond?

- Do I sense congruence in my life, or are there parts of my story that I prefer to keep hidden?

- How do I numb the longings of my mind, body and soul?

- What would be the cost to me to "live in the open," as suggested by Auguste Comte?

Chapter 7

Uncovering the Sacred

Perhaps I am stronger than I think. Perhaps I am afraid of my strength, and turn it against myself to make myself weak. Perhaps I am most afraid of the strength of God in me.
— *Thomas Merton*

Listen carefully...
— *opening words of the Rule of St. Benedict*

God does not see as human beings see; they look at appearances but God looks at the heart.
— *1 Samuel 16:7*

The great English poet Gerard Manley Hopkins begins one of his many sonnets with the line "The world is charged with the grandeur of God."[14] These words capture the experience of many as they look at the vastness of the prairies, the snow-capped peaks of the Rocky Mountains or the rugged coastlines of the great oceans. Yet many of us miss the sacred living deep within our core, and in the faces of the people around us.

Uncovering the sacred within the depths of being does not happen easily. For many, it takes a lifetime. We often feel that the sacred either is somewhere out there or is captured in images, experiences and words; the process of opening to the sacred within remains a difficult one for most of us.

Just after finishing a sabbatical at a university in Chicago, Pete arrived at my door at the Solitude of St. Joseph on the University of Notre Dame campus for an eight-day directed retreat. Each day, we would meet and talk about what was emerging from his time of prayer and solitude. After a couple of days, Pete walked into my office and shared a series of recurring dreams that he was having. Captured in aging notebooks, the dreams harkened back to the symbols, myths and rituals of his childhood in a remote part of New Mexico.

Pete was shaped as a youth by a system of values, cultural stories and myths indigenous to his culture, but had abandoned them in order to be part of the greater American dream. Shedding the stories and defining myths of his native culture that had given his inner and outer world meaning and purpose, Pete quickly embraced all things American. Yet meaning and fulfillment were elusive, despite his best attempts to fit in and be part of the collective story. After years of trying to fit into a different culture, Pete found himself working in the jungles of Central America with a remote group of Indians. These people reawakened within him his own culture and his unlived life.

What emerged during his retreat was a conscious choice to move back inside the depth of his being and meet the sacred as it was first revealed through his primal culture. By reviewing his dreams with me, sharing the stories of his culture and how they affected his life as a child and since, listening to the depths of his soul in quiet prayer, Pete knew that uncovering the sacred meant owning and valuing the depths of his uniqueness.

Pete's story told me that the gold within always seeks expression. We may wander far and wide from it, but the true self beckons us back to the depths of self over and over. Pete's story also reaffirmed for me the power of dreams as a way to reconnect to the deepest self. Dreams do not lie. Instead, they keep coming back in the same or different forms until we acknowledge them, respond and give them space to permeate our lives.

Pete's journey also reveals a path to discovering the sacred. Hopkins' sonnet "God's Grandeur" speaks of the "dearest freshness deep down," and it is this freshness that urges us to uncover layers of neglect and to risk, trusting in the power of the sacred to transform. Pete had to learn again that the culture from which he sprang was good. It was neither second rate nor inferior, just different from the dominant culture around him. Its stories, myths, rituals and way of life supposedly clashed with what constituted success and meaning in the larger world, so the first discovery Pete had to make was the richness of the culture that nourished. He could no longer reject the core of his being as lacking value. Instead, his primal myths gave him the key to meaning and purpose in today's world. In addition, he learned the importance of dreams to beckon us to deeper truths about life – something he had abandoned when he changed culture motifs. Yet in his original culture people talked freely of their dreams and respected the world of the spirit, unlike the highly rational culture in which he had immersed himself.

Finally, Pete had to learn to listen to and trust the voice within that urged him to become the person already living deep in his soul. Like the great spiritual master Benedict, who opened his Rule with the command to listen, Pete rediscovered the power to listen to the movements of the spirit inside him. Without this willingness to listen and respond, transformation cannot occur. It's always easy to gather more insight – but very difficult to turn the insight into concrete action.

Anne Gordon writes in *A Book of Saints* that "the call to spiritual life is a call to explore the uncharted seas of our heart…a call that cannot be answered without courageous spiritual independence."[15] Certainly Pete learned this lesson. All of us are invited to explore the uncharted seas of the heart. The question is, are we willing to do so? What will it take for us to open up and listen to the heart's tugging? When will we become attentive and responsive to our dreams? Of course, there's a cost if we choose to ignore the invitation. For Pete, the cost would have been gradual breakdown and ongoing unhappiness and frustration with his life and where it was headed. Luckily, for him, his retreat came at the end of a sabbatical year during which he had plenty of time to listen, reflect and explore. By concluding the year with the retreat, he found a way to bring the fragments of his life together in a new integration and then be on his way. Most of us are not so lucky as to have a sabbatical. Often, the wake-up call comes through illness, a broken relationship, the death of a loved one or friend, or an overwhelming experience of joy and love.

In the book of Deuteronomy in the Hebrew Scriptures, God talks about God's love for the Israelites, and says, "It is not in heaven, so that you need to wonder, 'Who will go up to heaven for us and bring it down to us, so that we may hear and keep it?'... No, the Word is very near to you, it is in your mouth and in your heart for your observance." (Deuteronomy 30:12-14) Just like Pete, we often need to let go of many of the things we thought made sense in order to rediscover the depths of the sacred within and without.

Andy's Story

When I met Andy he was 80 years old and dying of prostate cancer. His legs were so swollen the skin was bursting. He had been told by a number of physicians that there was nothing they could do to stop the swelling: when it got bad enough they would amputate his legs. In total frustration, Andy went to his barn and stuck cow catheters in his legs and scrotum in an effort to drain the fluid. Needless to say this was not effective. Andy's family physician, who was Czech, remembered that when she was a child people used to move fluid in the body through massage. She had recently learned of my manual lymphatic drainage work and referred Andy to me.

When Andy arrived at the clinic, he could barely climb the front stairs and was rapidly losing his ability to walk, even with the aid of a walker. Over the next seven days we drained five litres of fluid from Andy's legs. Unfortunately, his cancer was progressing and he was hospitalized in a small hospital 40 kilometres from the city. With his deteriorating condition I was not confident that my treatments could accomplish what Andy had set out to do.

Andy refused to stay in hospital because he wanted the edema (excess fluid) removed from his legs. He insisted that his family check him out of the hospital each day and drive him to our clinic. This trip was exhausting for Andy and his health further deteriorated. Because he was so determined to receive treatment and refused to allow the hospital staff to remove the bandaging used for the edema treatments, I agreed to travel to his hospital each day to work with him if his doctor could get permission from the hospital to allow the treatment. At this point his physician expected him to live only a few weeks, but Andy was determined to live long enough to return his legs to their original size and "show those doctors that something can be done for my legs so they won't tell someone else what they told me." For weeks Andy's legs continued to drain, although his condition necessitated continual edema treatment. Andy's overall health improved daily and the nursing staff noted that even when I worked on only one leg his overall condition would improve for a short time. Andy's health improved to the point that he was sent home with nursing care.

This meant that I had to drive daily to his trailer, which was even farther away than the hospital, but the only alternative was to abandon treatment and leave his legs to explode from the fluid build-up. There really was no choice. Although Andy was well enough to live at home with constant care, his cancer progressed and further medical complications worsened his edema. Months of daily treatment passed. Many times I lost confidence that we could achieve Andy's goal of returning his legs to their normal size, but he constantly encouraged me to continue to explore different approaches to draining his legs and healing his wounds.

Eventually Andy's legs approached their normal size. When this happened he commented, "I do not usually talk like this. I'm a welder, you know, but when you come to see me and walk through the door you bring an energy with you that you can see, and when you leave you leave some of it here with me." This was the beginning of a deepening in our relationship. From that point forward, Andy was more open with me and shared many experiences from his past – particularly those associated with Alcoholics Anonymous. The most significant comment he made, which I was later to learn was most important for his family, was this: "You know, for years I've gone to church and looked at the icons and listened to the sermons and never really believed, until one day I realized that Jesus Christ was real because he has been standing patiently beside my bed draining my legs day after day."

Sometimes the process of healing, even if we are dying, brings us to the recognition that the sacred lives and is evident in our daily lives. God, sacredness, divinity is not something to be pondered from a distance, or some powerful force that is separate from our own lives. It is not something that descends upon us to produce significant miracles. Instead, it is present in the little events that occur every day. Just as Andy found God through my work and shared the experience with me, I also found God in myself and recognized the divinity that lies within me, within Andy and within each and every one of us. God became present to those of us caring for Andy through our persistent struggle to reduce Andy's edema. God's presence shone through my doubts, through Andy's hope, faith and encouragement. Through the process of dying Andy uncovered the sacred.

Andy was not investing me with any shamanistic power and I don't purport to have any. Rather, he was recognizing that the sacred acts through people. God gifts each of us; each person is a conduit. Those gifts obviously vary. We each are graced in our own way. Although some people have a tendency to suggest that the healing professions hold a special kind of power, it is not true. The gift of aiding someone in his or her healing is no different than any other kind of gift – it is only a gift, and no more important than any other gift we are promised.

One of the things I learned through my experience with Andy was the importance of offering our gifts. Failing to do so disrespects the grace we are given. It is a great fault to withhold our gifts, even when we are unsure that they are adequate, when we doubt ourselves, when we presume that we are incapable of meeting the needs of the situation. To not offer our gifts because we may fail or because we feel inadequate is egotistical and suggests a lack of trust in the sacred.

Andy was able to return his legs to their normal size, but more importantly, lived long enough and gained enough awareness that he was able to reconcile a longstanding dispute with one of his sons. He died peacefully, having completed a spiritual journey that culminated in healing family relationships and finding a personal relationship with God.

Final Considerations

Uncovering the sacred within us can occur at any time in our lives. It can derive from the most innocent experience. Often we ignore its emergence or downplay recognition. We may be embarrassed to acknowledge the strength of God in our lives and the gifts that we are given. As Thomas Merton notes, "Perhaps I am most afraid of the strength of God in me."[16]

Uncovering the sacred in our lives challenges us to walk the spiritual journey we are called to. Like Pete, it challenges us to change, surrender, following the urgings of our soul to become not who we can imagine ourselves to be but who we are called to be.

In Andy's case, the sacred opened to a number of people during the process of his dying. Andy recognized the sacred in his everyday life and resolved painful issues within his family. His caregivers learned the value of using their gifts, regardless of their confidence in those gifts, and to trust that God works through each of us. Those who participated in his journey came to understand the presence of divinity within us all and the importance of opening to our calling.

Finally, the penetrating words of the Desert Mother Amma Syncletica capture the power of liberating the spark of the Divine within us. She writes, "In the beginning there is struggle and a lot of work for those who come near to God. But after that, there is indescribable joy. It is just like building a fire: at first it's smoky and your eyes water, but later you get the desired result. Thus, we ought to light the divine fire in ourselves with tears and effort."[17]

Questions for Reflection

- What in my life has a purpose larger than my self-interest?

- When have I been challenged to undertake an action or respond to a situation in which I am afraid?

- Where am I in pain, and from what might it stem?

- Which dreams, continual coincidences and subtle invitations in my life am I choosing to disregard?

- Whose presence or actions in my life inspire me to uncover and recognize the sacred?

- What connections do I see in my own life with Pete or Andy?

Chapter 8

Purging the Evil

Lies are always harmful to all things.

— *Leo Tolstoy*

It is dangerous to see the cause of evil outside of us because then repentance becomes impossible.

— *Frederick Robertson*

Repay evil with goodness.

—*The Talmud*

As a high school English teacher, I really enjoyed teaching *The Tragedy of Doctor Faustus* by Christopher Marlowe (1564–1593). This play portrays how Faustus sold his soul to the devil for the lure of pleasure and power. What made the teaching experience so enjoyable was that through drama we could explore the choices and motivations confronting us as humans. In earlier times and even today, the audience sees the good and bad angels seeking to persuade Faustus to follow their suggestions. The play's strength lies in the fact that we can all see ourselves struggling, just as Faustus did, in the struggle to choose what we really desire. We all know the power of seduction by evil, and how difficult embracing the good can be when both choices appear as good.

The audience of Marlowe's day understood clearly the power of evil to capture imagination and command actions. Today, we often pretend that evil does not exist – but it does. Evil can devour our energy, poison an atmosphere and destroy relationships with self, others and all Creation. It rarely reveals itself as bad. Instead, it dresses in the guise of good. Likewise, we can train ourselves not to see or recognize it. In the novel *Mark of an Angel,* by Nancy Houston, one of the characters poses a question all of us face. "Why should I tell her the true story instead of the made-up one? Just because it happens to be true? How does the truth concern her? Must she really be forced to learn it? Which truths are we required to pay attention to, and which can we ignore?"[18] Our challenge today lies in our ability to recognize how we co-operate with evil, can be seduced, overwhelmed and abused by it, or walk hand in hand with it.

While movies, video games and politics often identify one group as bad and another as good, the power of evil to overcome us lies within our hearts. Knowing ourselves and why we do something reveals how willingly we co-operate. I was sitting with a friend having a cup of coffee one day when she looked around the room, noticed someone and said, "There's the person who has tried to destroy me and others personally and professionally." Instantly, the coffee time became tense because of pain suffered due to the other's blatant envy and meanness.

What causes such evil to flow from our hearts and into the lives of those around us? A friend of mine once said that if we do not integrate the unlived parts of ourselves into our lives, we project our unhappiness upon others who live well. For instance, I once knew a person who had wanted to become a physician but circumstances did not permit it. Instead, he became a psychologist. When times had changed and one of his colleagues sought to become a physician, he fought against it. Why? Pure jealousy and unresolved anger, I suspect. He could not stand another having what he himself could not. Luckily, the person who wanted to become a physician succeeded in doing so and the psychologist swallowed his resentment and moved on with his life.

We all know that evil destroys. We understand the crippling power of intentional rejection, meanness of words and spirit, and cruel uses of position, power and authority to hurt another. At times we have participated in it, and at times we have been the recipients of its ugliness. Leo Tolstoy captures the challenge well when he writes, "Make an effort to do good things. It is even more important to make an effort to abstain from evil." Yet, it's more than effort. I once heard a sermon about the power of evil where the minister reminded us that only God can conquer evil. In confronting it, our choice is to co-operate with God's grace to move in the direction of the good or to succumb to evil in a way of life that ultimately diminishes us and others. On our own, I sense we are quite powerless to change evil into good. Yet, as those who survived the Nazi death camps and other horrendous experiences of cruelty and tangible evil realized, we can choose how we respond to the evil we encounter. We can either let it destroy and conquer us or we can choose a higher good. We can value ourselves enough not to be devoured and eaten alive by it, or we can succumb and be no different from those who have perpetrated the evil against us. The choice is always ours.

We can reflect upon the story of the testing of Jesus in the desert found in Luke 4. Jesus could have said yes to each of the three temptations put to him by the devil but instead, he turned the devil's words around. Finally, Scripture says, "Having exhausted all these ways of tempting him, the devil left him, to return at the appointed time." (Luke 4:13) Our lives are much the same. We struggle with the seductions of evil at home, work, in the community and in our hearts. Like Jesus, we need to find the courage to speak from the heart, know what is good and respond to it. Do we sometimes fail? Yes, we do. The challenge is to get up and start again. The temptation is to stay down when we stumble. History is filled with people making tough choices such as the choice to continue grappling with temptations that seek to diminish us. However, the very process shapes our lives, give us character and nurtures wisdom.

A Picture of Experiences: Ian

Purging the evil within can take many forms. I have worked with individuals who, following incidents in which they have been abused or have abused themselves or others, undertake a variety of purging rituals in an attempt to feel pure again. These rites have ranged from excessive dieting, exercise and massage to fasting, bulimia and colon cleanses. Some people perform the ritual consciously, some unconsciously. All seek some form of reconciliation that will lead to healing and wholeness.

I am reminded of Alan, who encountered a woman covered in blood in downtown Vancouver. She told Alan that she had just stabbed her friend and needed his help. She did not know where the friend was or what to do. Her first reaction was to flee. Alan, however, convinced her to accompany him to a nearby YMCA to call her mother and the police. While talking to her mother, the woman dropped the phone and ran off. Alan then called the police. After this encounter, Alan described a heavy, sick feeling that clung to him. Not knowing what else to do, he sought out a massage to rid himself of the darkness he felt. He felt that if he could let go of the woman's negative energy during the massage and open himself to the healing touch of the therapist, he would feel cleansed.

I am also familiar with fasting used in reconciliation. Over a four-year period I was able to fast under the direction of Native elders using traditional ceremony and ritual. This gave me the opportunity to observe individuals who have been both physically and sexually abused, as well as individuals who have abused others. Both groups used traditional Native methods of fasting as a step in the process of healing and forgiveness. Deep inside they hoped that in forgoing food, water and comfort and being in solitude with God for four days, they might be healed and returned to righteous lives. Through this ascetic practice, they sought to purge themselves of the devouring poison inside their very beings.

Beth's Story

Beth was a young woman who had suffered years of incest and sexual abuse from within and outside her family. She had done a lot of work to heal herself: she spent years in psychological counselling, attended support groups and had even written about her experiences. She told me, "I've been sexually abused much of my life and I think you can help me get it out of my body."

Her simple, straightforward observation challenged me to assist Beth in her desire to purge herself of the devouring evil. She recognized that massage could help her to find the hidden places within her body where she held the pain, as well as to face the pain and ask it to leave her. She knew the process would probably be painful for her and that we would have to go slowly. She also understood that in order to truly heal she would need to confront the evil within.

During our first few sessions Beth would not remove any clothing, even though she knew she would be completely draped in my presence. Over time, however, she began to feel safer and allowed me to massage her bare skin. The sessions were often emotional. Occasionally, she experienced flashbacks. Sometimes we would have to stop the session, and she regularly scheduled counselling following her massage – but she pressed on. She talked of her abuses, abusers and the painful shame she felt. The memories seemed to be found everywhere. I never knew where on her body, or when, we might trigger another memory. I often wondered if we'd ever find an end to the pain.

Over time, the sessions got easier for Beth and we uncovered fewer and fewer painful episodes. Some aspects of the massage even became relaxing as Beth came to terms with the hurt that had resided within her body. One day Beth told me about meeting one of her abusers by chance. She said she was interested to realize she was no longer afraid in his presence, although she was thankful the encounter occurred in a public place. This suggested to her that she had done a lot of healing. She felt that because the evil of his presence was resolved within her, she wasn't as afraid anymore.

Purging the evil within can be a frightening process. The courage shown by Beth and other sexual abuse survivors, both men and women, is incredible to witness. Their stories and the process they use to purge the evil within cause me to reflect on the value of locating any evil within us that remains after past encounters. I wonder what fears we each carry, and repeatedly experience, because we have not consciously faced our past and demanded that the residual energy of those experiences leave us. I wonder, too, if the residual energy of these past experiences provides a place for fear to reside, hate to grow and evil to dwell more easily in future.

I am reminded of a client who suffered for years as a child from an incestuous relationship. His greatest shame lay not in the incest but in the sexual exploitation to which he, in turn, subjected other children. While he understood that he had been only a child himself, and thereby unable to responsibly discern appropriate behaviour when the experiences were occurring, he suffered from the knowledge that he had participated in furthering the cycle of abuse.

In working with survivors of physical and sexual abuse, I sense that because the abuse affected the individual physically, emotionally and spiritually, the process of healing also needs to take those forms. In Beth's case, although she had done a great deal of work to heal intellectually and emotionally, she could not move on until she rid herself of the physical energy of those experiences remaining within. Forgiveness and reconciliation of self and others are an essential part of the healing process. It was only after Beth believed she had purged the evil from within her that she felt healed.

Final Considerations

Evil takes many forms and we deny a central core of our being if we do not acknowledge its power. Whether the evil stems from external encounters or from meeting our own evil desires, healing and reconciliation require active engagement with its insidious power to destroy and/or seduce. All the great spiritual traditions of the world identify the lure of evil as something that easily sidetracks our journey to wholeness. We must come to know ourselves, embrace the good and acknowledge the darkness within so that we can continue to grow and seek reconciliation with ourselves and others. As we reflect upon our lifelong struggle to choose the good, the sage wisdom of Abba Poemen comes to mind. Reflecting on the life of Abba Pior, Abba Poemen said, "Abba Pior made a fresh beginning every single day."[19]

The truism "There but for the grace of God, go I" rings out and challenges each of us to acknowledge that participation with evil is closer than we care to contemplate. We need to recognize and accept this fact, because as Frederick Robertson notes at the beginning of the chapter, it is dangerous to consider evil something outside of us because then repentance – and healing – is impossible. We like to turn a blind eye to evil and believe that our intentions and the intentions of those around us are always good, but honesty would tell us this is not always the case.

When we are not vigilant to the presence of evil in our daily lives, there is a tendency to become lax, rationalistic and even accepting of circumstances – as long as our own lives are not directly affected by corruption. It would be nice to believe that bad things, evil things, only happen in bad people's lives. However, the more honest we are in our reflection the more apparent it is that evil is present and available in most situations. Without constantly monitoring our thoughts and actions we can be easily corrupted by our own self-interest, greed and attachments. Without wanting to participate, we often inadvertently become involved in evil. We can, over time, lose sight of the light and our ability to discern. We become confused and lost in the dark. It's essential that we remain on guard, aware of evil's potential to deceive, and recognize that we can become complacent to its existence, particularly when it is not actively engaging us.

Questions for Reflection

- How does evil reveal itself to me?

- How have I been persuaded and/or coerced into participating with and perpetuating evil in my life?

- What rituals do I use to cleanse myself of actions I perceive as wrong or evil?

- When have I withheld forgiveness and reconciliation with others because I have not consciously faced experiences in my own past?

Chapter 9

Minding the Soul

The danger is not lest the soul should doubt there is any bread but lest by a lie, it should persuade itself that it is not hungry.

— Simone Weil

The body is the first student of the soul.

— Henry David Thoreau

In this culture, the soul and heart too often go homeless.

— Rachel Remen, MD

Only that day dawns to which we are fully awake.

— Henry David Thoreau

Over and over again in my work, I hear people say, "I just don't have any time." There is work to be done, children to be ferried here and there, an elderly relative to care for and large amounts of house and yard work. I am no different. I find it always easier to become immersed in the activities of the outer world than to stop and be mindful to what is moving inside of me.

Why is that, I wonder? What fear within wants me to keep busy, producing and active, and not listening? I sense at times that it's a fear of myself and who I am, and what lives deep inside of me. I guess it's the old saying – I am more comfortable with the monster I know than whatever and whoever lives deep inside. I am always struck by the example of a friend in San Francisco who thoroughly enjoys his solitude, that time when he can listen deeply to the stirrings of his soul and respond. I admire his mindfulness of action, and wish it could be more present within my own being.

In the annals of monastic journals in both the Christian and Buddhist traditions, the attitude of mindfulness dominates. Mindfulness, or consciousness, creates the inner space that allows us to hear, see and relate to the world inside ourselves as well as the world around us. Without mindfulness, we are driven and scattered in purpose and action.

In ancient Chinese literature the words of the Tao (translated as "the way" or "the path") capture the opportunity that mindfulness holds for each of us. This work also points out the dangers we quickly encounter if we do not care for ourselves in the midst of tending to others.

> Fill your bowl to the brim and it will spill.
> Keep sharpening your knife, and it will blunt.
> Chase after money and security
> and your heart will never unclench.
> Care about people's approval
> and you will be their prisoner.
> Do your work, then step back.
> It's the only way to serenity.[20]

This reflection from the Tao discusses the tension we all experience as we seek to live lives characterized by care for others, service and compassion. We can get too filled up with the other and miss our own needs, or chase after the wrong things and miss the hunger and unmet needs within our own lives. We can be so busy trying to make sure that others like us for what we do that we lose touch with who we are.

Much has been written about the need and responsibility to help one another. If we look into the great religious traditions, we see that certain traits enable people to be helpers without losing their balance. Mindfulness demands that we listen to what is moving inside of us and around us. Without the solitude needed to listen, we lose our focus. The great French philosopher Pascal wrote, "Many of our major problems derive from our inability to sit still in a room."[21] Over the years, I have shared Pascal's observation with many groups and people always acknowledge the truth of his insight. Yet in the same breath they often lament how difficult it is to sit still, given all the various outside interferences. The great saint and writer St. Benedict began his rule for monastic life, written over 1500 years ago, with the injunction "Listen." It is just as hard today as it was then. Yet it's at the core of a life well lived. In her insightful book *Illuminated Life*, Joan Chittister quotes from an elder who says this about silence: "Just as it is impossible to see your face in troubled water, so also the soul, unless it is clear of alien thoughts, is not able to pray to God in contemplation."[22]

Recently, when members of a group of people in the helping professions were asked what they were doing to care for themselves, very few had any clear answers. One or two said they kept a journal but most described their lives as hectic. In fact, self-care was last on their list of things to do. As people who care, we can give only what we have. If all we have to give is burnt-out energy, frustration and weariness, soon these feelings affect the people whose care is entrusted to us. Parker J. Palmer, a writer and speaker, said several years ago that one of the "shadows" or unconscious traits of leaders is that they believe they have to do everything. I suggest that many of us struggle with the same inner dynamic.[23] In his short essay/talk, which has appeared in a number of revisions over the years, Palmer challenges us to reflect upon our life and ask if we believe we must do everything. If we do, mindfulness disappears and broken relationships and burnout often occur.

Healing and attending to the needs of others demand a willingness to discover the sacred within ourselves and realize that without a balanced approach to our own lives true caring does not occur. We may mask some of the indicators of our own pain and discomfort through various soul-numbing activities, but real healing comes through a willingness to care for ourselves and become, in turn, "wounded healers." Today more than ever, in order to help others heal, we need to become people in which our own healing has begun.

Albert Camus once remarked, "In the depths of winter, I finally learned there within me lay an invincible summer."[24] That invincible summer will only be known when we make the time to listen and be mindful of what moves deep within us. And, as we move in this direction, we can begin to discern that which gives our life purpose, meaning and beauty and that which distracts and diminishes us. The decision to listen and mind the soul is ours, and no one else's.

Donavan's Story

Donavan, an Aboriginal, was in his mid-40s. He had spent the last three years in a northern Canadian community trying to help the people there recover from years of substance, physical and sexual abuse. When I was asked to see him, he hadn't slept in seven days. During the past year, his family had suffered three violent deaths and his sister had recently died from alcoholism on the street in a major Canadian city. While he was trying to help the aboriginal community, his own family was dying from the same circumstances he sought to correct. He grieved for them all.

Donavan's grief led to insomnia as he struggled intellectually and spiritually, day in and day out, to reconcile his efforts to help the broader community while his family had suffered and died. His body had responded to the pain in his soul and his desire for reconciliation by not sleeping. His friend called me because she thought the way to bring him back into balance was through his body. His friends, therapists and spiritual guides had not been able to reach him intellectually, emotionally or spiritually, so the physical approach presented the last opportunity. This seemed reasonable, as Thoreau's comment about the body being the first student of the soul reflects. Perhaps the soul could be reached through the body, and perhaps the teacher might listen to the student.

Donavan's massage seemed to be the appropriate intervention, as he commented that not only was his body relieved but that he felt that his spirit had been touched. His sleeping patterns returned to normal and he was able to work though his grief and return to his community development work with aboriginal people. In the months to come, he would return several times to see me when he felt that he had lost touch with his spirit. Each time, as he received a massage he would become grounded in his body and, in so doing, reconnect with his spirit. This seemed to come from his ability to focus on experiencing just what was occurring in the session; he forgot all else and became mindful of "now," able to be present "in the moment." Such an experience allowed him to let go and be mindful of "what is" and listen to what was moving within him.

Donavan understood one thing that many people do not, or are too afraid to face. People need to be able to find a safe place to take off their mask and expose their vulnerability in order to heal. He also understood that there is a relationship between body and spirit. He learned that in minding the soul, through reconnecting with his body he reconnected with his spirit. He learned that the body reflects "what is" much the same way a mirror does, without distortion or editing. What he experienced in life was experienced in his body, so to lose touch with his body was to lose touch with his life. In coming into an awareness of his body he became grounded again in who he was. This reconnection with our essential selves is an ongoing process, and one that is repeated time and again. In this day and age, it is increasingly easy to lose sight of self amid the many events taking place in our lives.

For Donavan, massage was a technique that put him back in touch with his spirit, forging anew the relationship between body and soul and bringing him to a mindful state – able to listen and experience reality for what it is. Massage is only one process for accomplishing this objective; many others exist that may be more appropriate to other people. However, whether the approach is massage, meditation, prayer, tai chi or another therapeutic approach, it is important for our ongoing health to keep body and soul connected and mindful of the present. If we do not mind our soul we suffer – spiritually, emotionally, intellectually and physically.

Wendy's Story

Wendy had been a professional nurse for over 20 years, caring for the sick, the injured and the dying. Now she herself was in pain. Like millions of North Americans she suffered back pain for which, in her case, there was no known cause. There had been nothing – no accident, incorrect lifting or degenerative disease – to explain why she should be experiencing debilitating pain intense enough to require her to be off work for months.

As we worked together over several months, Wendy's pain ebbed and flowed. Sometimes it would improve for a few days or a few hours, sometimes a week or more –

but it always seemed to return. Back pain wasn't her first physical warning of trouble, either. Over the last few years, she said, she had experienced facial pain, chronic sinus congestion and inflammation, headaches, fatigue and foot problems. In each case she was able to relate these ailments to some external factor that affected her at the time.

Wendy talked as we worked, and it became increasingly evident that there were many things bothering her. Her life had not always been rosy, and many things angered her. It took a period of subtle prompting, shared reflections and references to health and healing writers before Wendy connected the dots and realized that her pain was due to her anger. Once she did so, she sat down and composed a list of the things disturbing her, and woke the next morning free of pain. Although her pain returns on occasion, she has resumed working, is exercising and has begun psychotherapy to explore her compounded anger.

Before this point, Wendy hadn't bothered to take herself into account. She had constantly cared for the needs of others, to her own detriment. Wendy, like many in the healing professions, became consumed by her passion to help others. In the process she lost herself, and began to physically deteriorate and age without noticing. As a Native medicine man once told me after I fasted four days, "Drink before the others drink, for if you are without strength you cannot help others." Until her bodily pain became overwhelming, Wendy didn't address the things that bothered her. She just ignored them. She told herself her problems were not as important as those of the people around her.

Wendy began to heal when she realized that how she felt mattered, and that her body was signalling that the unresolved issues in her life needed attention. She healed when she became mindful of the root cause of her pain and stopped looking outside herself for the cure.

Wendy's experience causes me to think that what Thomas Merton said of contemplation can also be said of healing. To paraphrase Merton, those who make contemplation an object will be eternally separated from it because they are always holding it at arm's length to see if it is there.[25] Those who make healing an object will be separated as well. If we hold our suffering away from ourselves as something to be observed and assessed, we cannot fully participate in the healing process. To embrace our suffering, at its root, we will come to know who we are and subsequently heal. Tom Harpur, in *The Uncommon Touch*, notes: "Healing is more than an end, it is a means to a fuller life shared with the rest of humankind."[26] What we need to remember is that our own pain and healing matter just as much as anyone else's. To be a healing presence requires more than attending to the pain or suffering of others; it also demands being conscious and attending to one's own suffering.

This principle holds true whether we are engaged professionally in health services or whether we take on the role of being a healing presence within our families and relationships. Many people have long sacrificed their own health and well-being for those of others within their family or community. However, it is important to remember that there is a difference between true healing and just exchanging one form of suffering for another. To sacrifice oneself for another is not healing.

Final Considerations

Donavan and Wendy reveal how important silence, mindfulness and honesty are to healing. Both their life experiences reveal the truth of Pascal's observation, quoted in this chapter. True healing comes from being mindful of ourselves as well as others. It serves no one to mind the needs of others while ignoring ourselves. As Lama Surya Das has stated, "Mindfulness means attention and lucid awareness."[27] To not attend to our own needs or be consciously aware of ourselves within the context of the bigger picture fails to recognize the impact and implications of our own unmet hunger. Such an approach is not sustainable or healthy in the long term.

Our friends Wendy and Donovan learned the hard way that healing demands considering and honouring the gold within before we can reach out to others. In one of the parables in the Gospel according to Luke, Jesus captures the essence of minding the soul and how it relates to our life. He says:

> No one lights a lamp and puts it in some hidden place or under a tub, but on the lampstand so that people may see the light when they come in. The lamp of your body is your eye. When your eye is sound, your whole body too is filled

with light; but when it is diseased your body too will be all darkness. (Luke 11:33-36)

Questions for Reflection

- What is the role of solitude in my life?

- How do I find myself getting "sucked in" by the need to help others?

- What is healing for me in the midst of all my challenges?

- How can I integrate the words of the Native healer, "Drink before the others drink, for if you are without strength you cannot help others," into my life?

Part Three

Observations, Directions and Conclusions

Chapter 10

Healing as a Community

Try to reflect, in some corner of your mind, that the difficulties that surface in your life may be avenues toward greater understanding, no matter how improbable this seems at the time.

— *Avram Davis*

Healing demands the re-imaging of self and world, and it is not an easy task.

— *James Hollis*

Much of this book has been dedicated to concepts that relate to healing as individuals. It is only natural that we consider the healing experience from this perspective; however, we might also reflect on it from a more global view. Considering our personal journey in the context of a more shared experience, could it be a microcosm of a much larger human situation?

In the spring of the year 2000, I stood in the Tuol Sleng Detention Centre in the midst of the poverty, pain and suffering of Cambodia. I had come to be there because I had agreed to fly halfway around the world to assist an individual suffering from lymphedema. Once there, I felt compelled to seek out the darkness that had overwhelmed the country from 1976 to 1979 and examine the corruption of Cambodia's recent past and present. It felt as if God had withdrawn, lifting a veil to show me the impact of true evil. It was there, in the Killing Fields, that I pondered the insight of Avram Davis.[28] Although at that time I found it incomprehensible that the torture and murder of hundreds of thousands of people during the Khmer Rouge regime could be avenues to greater understanding, I soon realized that this was the case.

I also learned that healing from a shared pain can be a collective experience. I observed in utter amazement that the Cambodian people continued to move through their days without constantly feeling sorry for themselves. While there was an underlying acknowledgment of the pain that everyone had suffered, people generally lived in the present where they found joy, hope and renewal. Without discounting the suffering that had been experienced as a society, these people look to the future, seeking to right the wrongs of the past and move forward towards a healthier society.

Sometimes, as individuals, our personal journey gets caught up in the collective one. Although a personal avenue for understanding seems difficult to find in such horrific circumstances as genocide in Cambodia, the combined experience of the people creates a whole thoroughfare. In situations like this, we as a global community are challenged to learn. The individual experiences that make up the whole, while important to the individual and his or her loved ones, are overshadowed by the collective consciousness. As our spiritual journey unfolds in the community, so the community's path overlays our own – and at times may well supersede personal experience.

The pain of Cambodia, past and present, provides the opportunity for a much larger international community, as well as individuals such as myself, to clearly learn where darkness and neglect lead. The poverty, pain and suffering of the developing world, in all its many locations, mirror the spiritual emptiness of the industrialized nations and stand as a stark reminder that we all participate and share in the misfortunes of our brothers and sisters.

I use this example because seeing the impact of genocide and the contemporary suffering that followed from such a situation clearly demonstrated for me that the choices we make as individuals have a collective impact – positive or negative. They can contribute to healing or further the suffering of those affected. The spiritual journey of suffering and healing is always more than personal; it is an individual experience within a larger community.

Closer to home, I wonder if many of the illnesses, syndromes and diseases common today – such as chronic fatigue, fibromyalgia, heart disease and cancer – are not symptoms of a larger problem. I sense that until we begin to recognize that our society has been bent on being highly productive, results-driven and materialist – with possible consequences for our health – we will not heal. Without this acknowledgment and active steps to alleviate these societal pressures, many individuals will continue to fall prey to environmental illnesses.

It is possible that our collective journey as a society is the one most essential for healing. We need to recognize that it is our way of being in the world as a group that is causing individuals to fall ill. While we spend enormous amounts of money seeking medical cures for the individual diseases we face, we ignore those who suggest it is our lifestyle that is causing the problems. We heap enormous portions of our health care budgets on high-tech solutions, while little attention goes to addressing the physical, spiritual and emotional poverty within our communities that is contributing to the ill health of a considerable portion of society.

The way we live often predisposes us to the present-day illness we experience, but any voice that proposes such a notion is not well liked. That is because it challenges us to examine our lives and to shed activities, attitudes and goals that contribute to such illness. This may mean that the very fundamentals of our lives need to change. Unfortunately for many of us faced with the dilemma of refocusing, we generally continue to live as we always have, hoping to avoid the ill effects that crop up around us.

Day after day I see people living with pain in their lives; I live with my own. These people don't purposefully cause the pain they experience and they aren't always responsible for it, but regardless of how they acquire it, it is their pain and their challenge to heal themselves. Sometimes, to alleviate that suffering we must make choices that require us to step outside the accepted norms of our community. This may require us to shake off the materialistic values that are not supporting our wellness and embrace values that do enhance well-being. It may well mean addressing societal problems such as poverty, environmental pollution, stress and lifestyle choices that negatively impact many within our world.

Mary, a client, recently told me of an image she received that seems relevant to this discussion. In a massage session she wept deeply while I worked, but was unable to share her experience. As I held her head in my hands, she saw the image of humanity holding the earth in its hands. This confused Mary, as she did not understand its meaning in the context of her massage, nor the impact it would have on her. What her image reflects for me is the relationship between our individual and our collective healing journeys. Mary's image tells us that as we deal with our own pain we deal with our collective pain.

Her weeping reminded me of a statement by the Franciscan priest Richard Rohr: "Weeping leads to owning our complicity in the problem. Weeping is the opposite of blaming and also the opposite of denying. It leads to deep healing when inspired by the Spirit. When the weeping mode is lost, all our grief seems to turn into anger and accusation."[29] The most appropriate response to Mary's image, given our complicity in creating the current global situation, was, in fact, to weep. To blame, deny and make angry accusations leads nowhere; her image demonstrates that, collectively, we hold in our hands the ability to heal the pain of this world. We can take action – heal – by moving through "weeping for our complicity," individually and collectively.

Final Considerations

Healing as a community comes from respecting that our individual experiences may be components of a larger picture. It comes from accepting that each individual's health affects us all, and that we may be contributing to an individual's wellness or illness through the choices we make and the values that we uphold. To heal as a community we heal individually, but with collective respect for the individual's journey and collective support for individual choices that challenge our norms. We must be prepared to discuss the larger picture, to increase our collective awareness, and to address our spiritual emptiness.

We need to be careful to ensure that we are not importing pain and suffering into our daily lives merely for the sake of doing so. Awareness, clarity and sound judgment are important in discerning whether we play a part in the suffering of others. While it is easy to deny complicity, our role – however small or remote – is of value to our own well-being as well as that of others when we honestly assess our part in the collective suffering of our society. We must stop being like passersby at a highway accident, slowing down long enough to view the tragedy before speeding away, having learned nothing about driving more cautiously. To live this way is to live vicariously, to live without depth, on the surface of life viewing much, feeling little, changing nothing. For each of us, finding the balance between "bleeding without cause" and "owning your part" creates the environment necessary to "re-image our self and our world," as Hollis observes. In this way, we move appropriately towards healing as a community.

Questions for Reflection

- Who in my circle of relationships suffers for the collective pain of his or her family or community?

- How does the way I live contribute to the world's collective pain and suffering?

- What difficulties arise in my life that enable me to encounter greater awareness and understanding?

- Am I ready to face the possibility that the way I live my life predisposes me, and those around me, to illness? If not, how can I become ready?

- How can I shake off socially acceptable norms and values that do not support my wellness or address the sense of spiritual emptiness in and around me?

Chapter 11

Mind, Body and Soul: Integrating the Fragments of Our Lives

There are sparks of holiness in everything.
— *the Mezzeritzer rabbi*

Now I become myself.
It's taken time, many years and places.
I have been dissolved and shaken,
Worn other people's faces…
— Mary Sarton, *"Now I Become Myself"*

Each of us has to find the unity in which everything fits
and takes its right place.
Each must work out just what the right amount may be.
And it varies at different times of our life.
— *Thomas Merton*

Healing and integration do not occur overnight. Instead, the process of healing and integrating our mind, body and soul is a journey – not a destination. Too often we believe that if we eat the right food, see the correct therapist, pray the proper prayers and exercise daily, suddenly integration will pour in upon us. Unfortunately it happens neither so smoothly nor so easily. In fact, integration demands patience, effort and discipline, as well as support and guidance.

Throughout the history of various spiritual disciplines, spiritual guides have emerged to help people on the journey. A spiritual guide is someone, perhaps a mentor or a writer, who helps us ask the right questions about who our God is, what or who lives at our core, and how we find meaning and purpose in the midst of daily living. The spiritual guide does not provide answers, but helps us discover our way in the search for wholeness. The guide, it is to be hoped, speaks from personal experience and is aware of the paths of the soul through darkness and light, inertia and flexibility, sadness and joy, contentment and unease. Without this awareness, born of personal experience and study, a guide becomes dangerous to one's very soul. At their best, spiritual guides help us to integrate mind, body and soul as we continually seek to respond to inner hunger for congruence and wholeness.

If one cannot find a guide, learning to read and value an author who challenges us to deeper thinking and action becomes another means of understanding the journey. In the reading, we encounter mirrors of our specific journey as revealed in the lives of another. The lucky person finds not only a good guide but also a good set of writers to help us move through the labyrinths of our lives. As a teacher of spirituality, I have often felt the absolute hunger of people searching for good guides. When they are unable to find one, people often take classes in spirituality to see if there are others out there as hungry as they are. They're not disappointed. By finding others on a similar quest and some shared texts, people are often able to move forward and awaken the guide deep within their souls.

A friend took me aback when he once asked, "How are your spiritual practices?" It dawned on me that he was reminding me that practice provides the space and context for growth, development and learning to occur. It also creates the context of unlearning. Practice asks: Who am I reading, what is the quality of solitude in my life, how and when do I pray, and what about exercise, diet and study? My friend's question underscored for me how we make time for what we find most important. The issue is not about finding time but about making time. We all know the dilemma; now, how do we respond to the challenges that it poses? No one is free of this struggle. It is always easy to become distracted from the path of holiness and wholeness. We need to ask: do we know how we are seduced into distraction, and how it manifests itself in our daily living? If not, we have a lot to learn. Further, without stillness, we cannot listen to the depths of our mind, body and soul and discern the desires and messages hidden there.

As we move through life, we also need to acknowledge our mentors, those people whose very presence opens us to a larger sense of wonder and purpose within our own lives and enables us to understand our full potential. A mentor may be someone we know personally or someone whose presence can, in a single moment, awaken us to something much deeper within. I often ask groups, "Can you name one or more of your mentors?" Most people can. As we seek to integrate our body, mind and soul, we need to ask, who are our mentors? As we look at the broader community, who are the people we seek to emulate in our final years? And if we can identify them, how can we learn their secrets to a fulfilling life?

We may also have negative mentors – people whose way of life and being remind us that we do not want to go along that particular path. We see in them the unresolved demons of anger, resentment, regret, pain and suffering, and realize that if we do not engage our own demons we will end up like these people. The choice is ultimately ours, painful as it may be at times. The choice is between life and death. We need to keep asking ourselves what brings life/meaning into my life, and what brings death/rigidity and fear? The words of the great German poet Rainer Maria Rilke remind us of the impulse to integrate the fragments of our lives. He writes:

> I want to unfold
> I don't want to stay folded anywhere
> Because where I am folded
> There I am a lie.[30]

Intuitions from Ian's Practice

I have come to understand the Mezzeritizer rabbi's statement that "There are sparks of holiness in everything," not through words, reading or discussion but through experience, living in the present moment with others. Integrating the fragments of our lives occurs in the present. While it requires reconciling our past in some way, and being confident about carrying what we value into the future, integration can only take place in the present. It is only in the present moment that we can glimpse a "spark of holiness."

When I have accompanied some individuals along a portion of their spiritual journey, I have noted that the deep, lasting peace that comes from living a congruent, integrated life comes only with reconciling all parts of ourselves. We must be in tune, which means continually tuning, if we want to achieve harmony in mind, body and spirit. If issues or pain lie unresolved in any aspect of our being, we will not find and sustain lasting peace.

One of the problems we face in attaining this integrated state is that we are not consciously aware of ourselves. We continually encounter who we are in the midst of the ups and downs of living. It is this dynamic that moves us to constantly renew, reharmonize and re-evaluate, and it is through this process that we remain integrated. Integration is dynamic, as is peace; it is not a state that, once achieved, remains constant and unmoving. It requires vigilance, action and a willingness to change and stay in relationship with our world. Integration means responding to people and circumstances around us, meeting the challenge of the everyday and dealing with the deep, soul-searching questions that arise from our being.

Christ challenged his followers, through both his words and his actions, to be in the world – not of the world. We too are challenged to form whole, integrated selves engaged in our day-to-day lives without losing who we are to the values of a world we may not accept. For each of us, this means attaining clarity about all aspects of ourselves, so that we may freely respond to the world around us, accepting what fits and rejecting what does not. Without intimately knowing and accepting all aspects of ourselves we get lost in responding, taking on attitudes, values and behaviours that are not congruent with who we are. We are soon lost, uncertain about who we really are and what we truly believe. We become the mask and costumes we wear to impress each other, and lose touch with the true self behind the actor. Our lives become fragmented.

My own life bears this out. For years I functioned successfully as a public sector manager, then as a management consultant flying about the country restructuring organizations and installing automated systems to improve work performance. While this work was valued and contributed positively to many people's lives, it did not fulfill mine. I made some money. I stayed in the best hotels, ate in the finest restaurants and lived a lifestyle that appeared successful, but at the same time I grew more and more unhappy. I worked constantly, visited home a few days a month and was increasingly absent from my family until one day my three-year-old daughter said, "Are you going to visit me again today, Daddy?" As the saying goes, "out of the mouths of babes" came the truth I needed to hear. I realized I was only a visitor in the lives of my wife and child, and in all likelihood only a visitor in my own.

I had gotten lost along the way, listening intently to how society defined success while failing to integrate significant aspects of myself. My life became incongruent with values I held, and I lost touch with my soul. Nine words from a toddler changed all that. I went home to the ocean where I grew up, and with the help of my wife figured out what I valued, what I wanted from my work and how I wanted to live. When we returned home I quit the consulting business, sold our house and returned to school to become a massage therapist. Through this journey I have begun bringing together the previously fragmented areas of my life. Like the stories of others we have shared in this book, I am attempting to live in a more integrated fashion, remaining vigilant to the changing dynamics reflected in my mind, body and soul. I want to live in wholeness and not get lost again.

For each of us, this process takes its own form. I remember a client recently commenting that the bodywork she was experiencing was surprisingly transforming. The sessions resulted in her receiving numerous images and memories that came from deep within. Her reflection was that she was somehow remembering her body and her life experience. Her sense was that as she did, she felt that others were remembering her. As she recalled her past and reformed it within her present context she moved towards integration and peace in her life. She brought the previously fragmented aspects of who she was into an integrated whole, within the present. What she learned from each experience was acknowledged; joys were accepted and pains were released. Experiences did not have to be denied or rejected; they found a place in her present circumstances.

Her experience gave me an analogy. I believe we move through life collecting individual pieces of a three-dimensional jigsaw puzzle without knowing what picture is being formed. As we integrate the fragments of our lives we place the pieces in their proper place, and the picture of who we are – based on each individual experience – becomes clear. All the pieces have an important place in forming who we are. If any pieces are left out, the picture is not complete. I read once that we are but a word uttered by God; what that word is depends on how we respond to God's call. We do not know the word or the picture until much later, after we have responded to God's presence in our lives.

It has been my experience that in order for someone to accomplish this integration he or she must stay in the pain and suffering long enough to know what it is. This does not mean that it is necessary to relive every detail or move into the pain to the point of retraumatizing the individual; we must simply acknowledge that we are in pain in order to sort out what is bothering us. Richard Rohr comments,

> We mustn't engineer an answer too quickly. We must not get too settled too fast. We can easily manufacture an answer to take away the anxiety. To stay in God's hands, to trust, means that to a certain degree I have to stop taking hold myself. I have to hold, instead, a degree of uncertainty, fear, and tension. What must be sacrificed, and it will feel like a sacrifice, is the attachment and the strange satisfaction that problem-solving gives us. We must not get rid of the anxiety until we have learned what it wants to teach us.[31]

Our society is too quick to seek a cure without truly healing. We just want to be away from pain, and we want the people around us to be pain-free as well. We want this so much that we are willing to mask the symptoms without trying to deal with its cause. To use the puzzle analogy, if the pieces, which are unresolved pain, are painted black, we can't see that part of the puzzle. If enough pieces are black, the whole picture is obscured and unrecognizable. If we live with enough unresolved pain in our lives, if our lives remain fragmented and pieces of self are incongruent with the whole being, we will not come to know who we are. We will spend our lives longing for wholeness rather than achieving it.

Final Considerations

Rabbi Harold S. Kushner, in his book *Living a Life That Matters*, identifies the struggle all of us encounter in seeking to integrate our life. He writes,

> When we defeat the still, small voice of God inside us, we lose. But that voice inside us will not be stilled forever.... It will find a time when we are vulnerable. It will attack us at a weak moment. And when the struggle is over, we will like Jacob/Israel be bruised and limping. But again, like Jacob, we will be whole, we will be at peace with ourselves, in a way we never were before.[32]

The path to integration is not unlike the path Jacob took in the Scriptures. There are lessons along the way, there are successes and failures and wrestling with our inner selves as we seek to better know ourselves and our purpose in life. We must hope that, like Jacob, we remain attuned to the voice of God deep within us, and meet people along the way who can challenge and support us in our journey. And we too must wrestle with the angel through the night, so we may emerge with a new sense of who we are and where we are going.

Questions for Reflection

- What are my spiritual practices?

- Who are my mentors and how do they guide me today?

- What does doing God's will mean to me at this time in my life?

- What must I do to honour and value the life I have been given?

- Where do I find hope in my life?

Epilogue

The longing for wholeness shapes our lives whether or not we are conscious of it. Not too long ago, when I was giving a talk entitled "Ethics, Spirituality and Intimacy: The Search for Wholeness," I asked participants why they chose this presentation over another one. The dominant response centred on the words "the search for wholeness." What is it that pushes away inside of us, that can never be fully satisfied? Deep within, I sense it is this longing for wholeness and a connection to the deepest parts of ourselves, the world around us and the sacred who lives within and among us.

Writer and psychoanalyst James Hollis claims in many of his writings that Carl Jung believed that "our deepest need is for a sense of spiritual or psychic locus." By this Jung means that we all desire connection to something larger than ourselves that gives us a sense of belonging, purpose and destiny. Over and over in our own work, this insight has been confirmed for Ian and me. As humans, we hunger and long for something more than meets the eye. Unfortunately, sometimes our longing goes awry and we find ourselves fragmented physically, emotionally, spiritually and psychologically.

As case studies have shown, the path to wholeness often demands a willingness to travel through a great deal of darkness, letting go of our inner demons and ambiguity. Hollis, in his book *Swamplands of the Soul*, captures the significance of the journey by reflecting upon Hindu spirituality. He writes,

> Hindus say the world is God's play. The vision of transcendence may not be clear, but the task of catching glimpses, hatching new eggs along the way, suffering the arid places of the soul, leads in the end to the realization that the meaning is not in the arrival but in the journey itself. That is the wisdom of a person who 'goes through.'[33]

Recently I sat with a friend who was sharing some of his frustrations about life and a deep sense of aloneness in the path he had not really chosen for himself. Months before, he had held a very public position; now, through a merger, he found himself exploring a new career. Within this context we talked about fear and the grip it had upon his life. I then shared with him a passage from James Hollis' *The Archetypal Imagination*, in which he remarks that "what blocks each of us is fear – the fear of loneliness, fear of rejection, and most of all, fear of largeness."[34] His eyes lit up and said, "Yes, I agree!" Hollis describes the angst of many of us. On one hand we long for wholeness, while on the other fear holds us back from being the person we are called to be. T.S. Eliot, in the final words of his play *Murder in the Cathedral*, speaks of our fear of the power of the sacred to shape our lives. He writes, "Men fear fire and men fear flood and men fear pestilence; but more than anything else they fear the love of God." Yet we long for wholeness.

The commitment to live with integrity, a sense of purpose and meaning is not a straight line. Instead, it's a journey of successes and failures, forgiveness and reconciliation and joy and blessing. In the midst of it, we need to be open to the urgings of soul and what it seeks of us. We close with the profound words of Albert Schweitzer, who captures the tension of all who long for wholeness.

> You know of the disease in Central Africa called sleeping sickness…. There also exists a sleeping sickness of the soul. Its most dangerous aspect is that one is unaware of its coming. That is why you have to be careful. As soon as you notice the slightest sign of indifference, the moment you become aware of the loss of a certain seriousness, of longing, of enthusiasm and zest, take it as a warning. You should realize your soul suffers if you live superficially.[35]

Selected Reading

Bolen, Jean Shinoda, MD. *Ring of Power: The Abandoned Child, the Authoritarian Father, and the Disempowered Feminine*. New York: HarperSanFrancisco, 1992.

———. *Close to the Bone: Life-Threatening Illness and the Search for Meaning*. New York: Scribner. 1996.

———. *Crossing to Avalon: A Woman's Midlife Pilgrimage*. New York: HarperSanFrancisco, 1994.

Burton-Christie, Douglas. *The Word in the Desert: Scripture and the Quest for Holiness in Early Christian Monasticism*. New York: Oxford Press, 1993.

Carlson, Richard and Benjamin Shield. *Handbook for the Soul*. Boston: Little, Brown and Company, 1995.

Chittister, Joan. *A Passion for Life: Fragments of the Face of God*. Maryknoll: Orbis Books, 1996.

———. *The Rule of St. Benedict: Insights for the Ages*. New York: Crossroad, 1997.

———. *Illuminated Life: Monastic Wisdom for Seekers of Light*. Maryknoll, New York: Orbis Books, 2001.

Coelho, Paulo. *The Alchemist*. New York: HarperSanFrancisco, 1994.

———. *The Fifth Mountain*. New York: Harper Perennial, 1998.

Cooper, David A. *God Is a Verb: Kabbalah and the Practice of Mystical Judaism*. New York: Riverhead Books, 1997.

Das, Lama Surya. *Awakening the Buddha Within: Tibetan Wisdom for the Western World*. New York: Broadway Books, 1997.

Davis, Avram. *The Way of Flame: A Guide to the Forgotten Mystical Tradition of Jewish Meditation*. New York: HarperSanFrancisco, 1996.

Davis, Avram and Manuela Dunn Mascetti. *Judaic Mysticism*. New York: Hyperion, 1997.

de Mello, Anthony. *Awareness*. New York: Doubleday, 1990.

———. *The Way to Love*. New York: Doubleday, 1991.

De Wall, Esther. *A Seven Day Retreat with Thomas Merton*. Ann Arbor, MI: Servant Publications, 1992.

Dossey, Larry. *Healing Words: The Power of Prayer and the Practice of Medicine*. New York: Harper SanFrancisco, 1993.

Edinger, Edward F. *The Bible and the Psyche: Individuation Symbolism in the Old Testament*. Toronto: Inner City Books, 1986.

Fox, Matthew. *Original Blessing: A Primer in Creation Spirituality*. Santa Fe: Bear & Co., 1983.

France, Peter. *Hermits: The Insights of Solitude*. New York: St. Martin's Press, 1996.

Gilmartin, Richard J. *Pursuing Wellness: Finding Spirituality*. Mystic, CT: Twenty-Third Publications, 1996.

Gordon, Anne. *A Book of Saints: True Stories of How They Touch Our Lives*. New York: Bantam Books, 1994.

Hammarskjöld, Dag (translated by Leif Sjoberg & W.H. Auden). *Markings*. New York: Alfred A. Knopf, 1972.

Hanh, Thich Nhat. *The Heart of the Buddha's Teaching*. New York: Broadway Books, 1998.

———. *Living Buddha Living Christ*. New York: Riverhead Books, 1995.

———. *Peace Is Every Step*. New York: Bantam Books, 1991.

Harpur, Tom. *The Uncommon Touch: An Investigation of Spiritual Healing*. Toronto: McClelland & Stewart, 1995.

———. *Prayer: The Hidden Fire*. Kelowna, B.C.: Northstone Books, 1998.

Hart, Patrick and Jonathan Montaldo. *The Intimate Merton: His Life from His Journals*. New York: HarperSanFrancisco, 1999.

Heschel, Abraham Joshua. *Moral Grandeur and Spiritual Audacity*. New York: Farrar, Straus and Giroux, 1996.

Hillman, James. *The Force of Character and the Lasting Life*. New York: Random House, 1999.

———. *The Soul's Code: In Search of Character and Calling*. New York: Random House, 1996.

Hollis, James. *Creating a Life: Finding Your Individual Path*. Toronto: Inner City Books, 2001.

———. *Swamplands of the Soul: New Life in Dismal Places*. Toronto: Inner City Books, 1996.

———. *The Eden Project: A Jungian Perspective on Relationship*. Toronto: Inner City Books, 1998.

———. *The Archetypal Imagination*. College Station, TX: Texas A & M University Press, 2000.

Jaffe, Lawrence W. *Celebrating Soul: Preparing for the New Religion*. Toronto: Inner City Books, 1999.

The Jerusalem Bible: Reader's Edition. Garden City, NY: Doubleday, 1968.

Johnson, Robert. *The Fisher King & The Handless Maiden: Understanding the Wounded Feeling Function in Masculine and Feminine Psychology*. New York: HarperSanFrancisco, 1993.

Johnson, Robert A. with Jerry M. Ruhl. *Balancing Health and Earth: A Memoir of Visions, Dreams, and Realizations*. New York: HarperSanFrancisco, 1998.

Kearney, Michael, MD. *Mortally Wounded: Stories of Soul Pain, Death and Healing*. New York: Touchstone Book, 1996.

———. *A Place of Healing: Working with Suffering in Living and Dying*. Oxford, England: Oxford Press, 2000.

Keen, Sam and Anne Valley-Fox. *Your Mythic Journey Through Writing and Storytelling*. Los Angeles: Jeremey P. Tarcher, Inc., 1973.

Kornfield, Jack. *After the Ecstasy, the Laundry*. New York: Bantam Books, 2000.

Kushner, Harold S. *Living a Life that Matters: Resolving the Conflict Between Conscience and Success*. New York: Alfred K. Knopf, 2001.

Lane, Belden C. *The Solace of Fierce Landscapes: Exploring Desert and Mountain Spirituality*. New York: Oxford, 1998.

Lawrence, Brother (translated by Edmonson, Robert J.). *The Practice of the Presence of God*. Brewster, MA: Paraclete Press, 1985.

Leech, Kenneth. *Soul Friend: The Practice of Christian Spirituality*. San Francisco: Harper & Row Publishers, 1977.

May, Rollo. *The Courage to Create*. New York: Bantam, 1975.

Miller, Alice. *The Truth Will Set You Free: Overcoming Emotional Blindness and Finding Your True Adult Self*. New York: Basic Books, 2001.

Moyers, Bill. *Healing and the Mind*. New York: Doubleday, 1993.

Nouwen, Henri. *Reaching Out*. New York: Doubleday, 1975.

―――. *The Inner Voice of Love: A Journey Through Anguish to Freedom*. New York: Doubleday, 1996.

―――. *The Return of the Prodigal Son: A Meditation on Fathers, Brothers and Sisters*. New York: Doubleday, 1992.

Ornish, Dean, MD. *Love & Survival: The Scientific Basis for the Healing Power of Intimacy*. New York: HarperCollinsPublishers, 1998.

Pagels, Elaine. *The Gnostic Gospels*. New York: Vintage Books Edition, 1981.

Palmer, Parker. *Let Your Life Speak: Listening for the Voice of Vocation*. San Francisco: Jossey-Bass, 2000.

Remen, Rachel, MD. *My Grandfather's Blessings: Stories of Strength, Refuge and Belonging*. New York: Riverhead Books, 2000.

―――. *Kitchen Table Wisdom: Stories that Heal*. New York: Riverhead Books, 1996.

Ripple, Paula. *Growing Strong in Broken Places*. Notre Dame, IN: Ave Maria Press, 1986.

Rohr, Richard. *Everything Belongs*. New York: Crossroads, 1999.

————. *Simplicity: The Art of Living*. New York: Crossroad, 1991.

Rupp, Joyce. *The Cup of Our Life: A Guide for Spiritual Growth*. Notre Dame, IN: Ave Maria Press, 1997.

Sanford, John A. *Healing and Wholeness*. New York: Paulist Press, 1977.

————. *Evil: The Shadow Side of Reality*. New York: Crossroad, 1982.

Shannon, William H. (ed.). *Thomas Merton – The Hidden Ground of Love: Letters*. New York: Farrar, Straus, Giroux, 1985.

Stella, Tom. *The God Instinct: Heeding Your Heart's Unrest*. Notre Dame, IN: Sorin Books, 2001.

Thompson, C. Michael. *The Congruent Life: Following the Inward Path to Fulfilling Work and Inspired Leadership*. San Francisco: Jossey-Bass Publishers, 2000.

Thoreau, Henry David. *Walden*. Toronto: Random House Canada, 1992.

Toibin, Colm. *The Story of the Night*. Toronto: McClelland & Stewart, 1997.

Tolstoy, Leo (translated by Peter Sekrin). *A Calendar of Wisdom: Wise Thoughts for Every Day*. London: Hodder & Stoughton, 1998.

Thompson, Gretchen. *God Knows Caregiving Can Pull You Apart: 12 Ways to Keep It Together*. Notre Dame, IN: Sorin Books, 2002.

Waddell, Helen. *The Desert Fathers*. New York: Vintage Books, 1998.

Welch, John. *Spiritual Pilgrims: Carl Jung & Teresa of Avila*. New York: Paulist Press, 1982.

———. *When Gods Die: An Introduction to John of the Cross*. New York: Paulist Press, 1990.

Whyte, David. *The Heart Aroused: Poetry and the Preservation of the Soul in Corporate America*. New York: Doubleday, 1994.

———. *Crossing the Unknown Sea: Work as a Pilgrimage of Identity*. New York: Riverhead Books, 2000.

Notes

1 Bill Moyers, *Healing and the Mind* (New York: Doubleday, 1993), 5.

2 Brother Lawrence, "Practices Necessary to Acquire the Spiritual Life," in *The Practice of the Presence of God*, Robert J. Edmonson, trans. (Brewster, MA: Paraclete Press, 1985), 125.

3 James Hollis, *Swamplands of the Soul: New Life in Dismal Places* (Toronto: Inner City Books, 1996), 29.

4 Bill Moyers, *Healing and the Mind*, 351.

5 James Hollis, *The Eden Project: In Search of the Magical Other* (Toronto: Inner City Books, 1998), 130, quoting W.H. Auden.

6 C. Michael Thompson, *The Congruent Life* (San Francisco: Jossey-Bass Publishers, 2000), 151, quoting Gandhi.

7 Joan Chittister, *Illuminated Life: Monastic Wisdom for Seekers of Light* (Maryknoll, New York: Orbis, 2000), 87.

8 Peter France, *Hermits* (New York: St. Martin's Press, 1996), 207, quoting Robert Lax.

9 Sam Keen and Anne Valley-Fox, *Your Mythic Journey Through Writing and Storytelling* (Los Angeles: Jeremy P. Tarcher Inc., 1973), 11, quoting Juan Ramon Jiminez.

10 Leo Tolstoy (translated by Peter Sekrin), *The Calendar of Wisdom* (London: Hodder & Stoughton, 1997), 335.

11 Chittister, *Illuminated Life*, 54.

Notes

[12] Robert Frost, "The Road Not Taken," in *The Road Not Taken: A Selection of Robert Frost's Poems* (New York: Henry Holt, 1995), lines 18-20.

[13] Chittister, *Illuminated Life*, 59.

[14] Gerard Manley Hopkins, "God's Grandeur," in *Gerard Manley Hopkins: The Major Works* (Toronto: Oxford University Press, 2002), line 1.

[15] Anne Gordon, *A Book of Saints: True Stories of How They Touch Our Lives* (New York: Bantam Books, 1994), 40.

[16] Patrick Hart and Jonathan Montaldo, eds., *The Intimate Merton: His Life from His Journals*, New York: HarperSanFrancisco, 1999, 164.

[17] Chittister, *Illuminated Life*, 40.

[18] Nancy Huston, *The Mark of the Angel* (South Royalton, VT: Steerforth Books, 1999), 16.

[19] Chittister, *Illuminated Life*, 35.

[20] Joan Chittister, *The Rule of St. Benedict: Insight for the Ages* (New York: Crossroad, 1997), 36, quoting the Tao Te Ching.

[21] Belden C. Lane, *The Solace of Fierce Landscapes* (New York: Oxford, 1998), 205, quoting Pascal.

[22] Chittister, *Illuminated Life*, 105.

[23] Parker J. Palmer, *Leading from Within: Reflections on Spirituality and Leadership* (Indianapolis, IN: Office of Campus Ministries), 14.

[24] Philip Phody, ed., "Return to Tipasa," in *Lyrical and Critical Essays* (New York: Knopf, 1968), 169.

[25] Thomas Merton, *The Hidden Ground of Love* (Farrar, Straus, Giroux, 1985), 346.

[26] Tom Harpur, *The Uncommon Touch: An Investigation of Spiritual Healing* (Toronto: McClelland & Stewart, 199...), 237.

[27] Lama Surya Das, *Awakening the Buddha Within: Tibetan Wisdom for the Western World* (New York: Broadway Books, 1997), 305.

28 Avram Davis, *The Way of Flame: A Guide to the Forgotten Mystical Tradition of Jewish Meditation* (New York: HarperSanFrancisco, 1996), 89.

29 Richard Rohr, *Everything Belongs* (New York: Crossroads, 1999), 126.

30 Paula Ripple, *Growing Strong at Broken Places* (Notre Dame, IN: Ave Maria Press, 1986), 87, quoting Rainer Marie Rilke.

31 Rohr, *Everything Belongs,* 112.

32 Harold S. Kushner, *Living a Life That Matters: Resolving the Conflict Between Conscience and Success* (New York: Alfred A. Knopf, 2001), 34.

33 James Hollis, *Swamplands of the Soul,* 138.

34 James Hollis, *The Archetypal Imagination* (College Station, TX: Texas A & M University Press, 2000), 104.

35 Richard Carlson and Benjamin Shield, *Handbook of the Soul* (Boston: Little, Brown & Company, 1995), 85, quoting Albert Schweitzer.

AGMV Marquis

MEMBER OF SCABRINI MEDIA

Quebec, Canada
2003